THE CHALLENGES OF GOVERNANCE IN A COMPLEX WORLD

THE CHALLENGES OF GOVERNANCE IN A COMPLEX WORLD

To Michael Pawlyn

Thank you for your support.

With best wishes
from Peter Ho
October 2018

PETER HO

Published by

World Scientific Publishing Co. Pte. Ltd.

5 Toh Tuck Link, Singapore 596224

USA office: 27 Warren Street, Suite 401-402, Hackensack, NJ 07601

UK office: 57 Shelton Street, Covent Garden, London WC2H 9HE

British Library Cataloguing-in-Publication Data
A catalogue record for this book is available from the British Library.

THE CHALLENGES OF GOVERNANCE IN A COMPLEX WORLD

ISBN 978-981-3231-82-5
ISBN 978-981-3233-74-4 (pbk)

For any available supplementary material, please visit
http://www.worldscientific.com/worldscibooks/10.1142/10759#t=suppl

Desk Editor: Sandhya Venkatesh

Typeset by Stallion Press
Email: enquiries@stallionpress.com

Printed in Singapore

THE S R NATHAN FELLOWSHIP FOR THE STUDY OF SINGAPORE
AND THE IPS-NATHAN LECTURE SERIES

The S R Nathan Fellowship for the Study of Singapore was established by the Institute of Policy Studies (IPS) in 2013 to support research on public policy and governance issues. With the generous contributions of individual and corporate donors, and a matching government grant, IPS raised around S$5.9 million to endow the Fellowship.

Each S R Nathan Fellow, appointed under the Fellowship, delivers a series of IPS-Nathan Lectures during his or her term. These public lectures aim to promote public understanding and discourse on issues of critical national interest.

The Fellowship is named after Singapore's sixth and longest-serving President, the late S R Nathan, in recognition of his lifetime of service to Singapore.

Other books in the IPS-Nathan Lecture series:

The Ocean in a Drop – Singapore: The Next Fifty Years
by Ho Kwon Ping
Dealing with an Ambiguous World
by Bilahari Kausikan

CONTENTS

FOREWORD

A *Kopitiam* Karol[1]

A sacred cow, a *black elephant* and a *black swan*[2] were sitting in a *kopitiam* on an unnamed street in Singapore. The sacred cow loudly moo'ed for a *kopi-o*, the black elephant trumpeted for a *teh tarik*, and the black swan honked for a cappuccino.[3] Then they started talking.

The sacred cow, sleek, smug and self-satisfied, boasted, "I am the spirit of Singapore past. Everyone worships me. I made Singapore a huge success. Who can argue with success?"

Not wanting to be outdone, the black elephant stood up, an imposing presence that cast a large shadow over the table. He looked pointedly towards the sacred cow and boomed out, "You are so yesterday! I am the spirit of Singapore present. Everyone sees me, yet they let me do whatever I want. I hold such a power over people. No one stands in my way."

The black swan then spoke with quiet menace, "Both of you are irredeemable. You are beyond hope. I am the real spirit of Singapore yet to come.

---

[1] With apologies to Charles Dickens.

[2] Nassim Nicholas Taleb described rare, hard-to-predict and game-changing events as *black swans*. The black elephant is my metaphor for a mutant "elephant in the room" that everyone pretends not to notice until it blows up as a problem, and then everyone calls it a black swan.

[3] *Kopitiam* is a casual local coffee shop, serving popular drinks like *kopi-o* (sweetened black coffee) and *teh tarik* (sweetened tea with milk with a distinctive frothy top).

When I arrive, both of you will count for nothing, because I will unleash new, unknown and powerful forces that you cannot even imagine!"

Hearing this noisy argument, the kopitiam owner, Buay Tahan,[4] came up and said, "Stop talking nonsense! None of you deserve a seat in my kopitiam. Mr Sacred Cow, you did not make our past! It was through the hard work of all Singaporeans that together we overcame our difficulties. We dared to defy conventional wisdom and take risks, to create the Singapore story. Mr Black Elephant, we know who you are! You belong in a zoo. Singaporeans are practical and pragmatic people. We are not fools. We will find you and your kind, lock you up, and throw away the key."

Buay Tahan continued, "Mr Black Swan, I respect you, because you are the most dangerous of the lot. But we have learnt from dealing with the likes of Mr Sacred Cow and Mr Black Elephant that, despite the dangers that you pose, there is always opportunity if we are only brave enough to take the future into our own hands, imagine new possibilities and new worlds, and commit ourselves through action to translating hope into reality."

And with that, the sacred cow and the black elephant faded away. Only the black swan remained, nursing his cappuccino and pondering what he ought to do next. Buay Tahan then spoke directly to the black swan, and declared in a clear voice, "Out with you. It is no longer business as usual. We are going to embrace change, because our future depends on it. We know that there are no guarantees for the future, but we are prepared to take and manage the risks of creating a Singapore of the future that is worthy of our forefathers."

On hearing that, the black swan flew out of the kopitiam, tracing a morose path, never to be seen again.

Thus ends the Kopitiam Karol, a fable of modern Singapore that compresses the essence of the four lectures contained in this book into a few paragraphs.

But of course, this fable carries the risk of oversimplification.

The modern public policy enterprise rests on four assumptions. First, the assumption of *predictable order*, where cause leads to effect. Second,

---

[4] *Buay Tahan* is a Singlish expression of frustration, meaning that one is unable to put up with something.

the assumption of *reductionism*,[5] which lends itself to a "divide and rule" approach, and explains the proliferation of agencies and bureaucracies as a standard response to emerging problems. Third, the assumption of *linearity*, that the past is prologue, and that the future is merely the present, plus or minus (x)per cent. And finally, that the public policy enterprise is *mechanistic*, where problems are unambiguous and solutions are optimal.

But complexity — particularly increasing complexity that defines the world we live in today — weakens the basis for all these four assumptions. This presents a huge challenge for governments and for good governance.

In an increasingly complex world, emergence, disruption and black swans are sources of anxiety. It is easy to feel helpless, as if we were flailing in ocean currents beyond our control. The geographer David Harvey, and Karl Marx before him, talked about "the annihilation of space by time"[6] by emerging technologies and new ways of organising. Not only are connections and feedback loops denser than before, the speeding up and the compression of the world through globalisation, urbanisation, and the Internet make it seem as though the future is hurtling uncontrollably towards the present. We are no longer faced with Alvin Toffler's "future shock",[7] but the much more immediate present shock. Thinking about the future becomes very challenging when all our bandwidth is taken up in trying to cope with the surprises of today and changes in the present. Taking refuge in sacred cows and ignoring black elephants are some of the faulty responses resulting from an environment of increasing complexity and accelerating change.

An energetic spirit of courage and innovation transformed Singapore from Third World to First within two generations. But the road to the future cuts through the past and the present. The innovations of one generation

---

[5] Reductionism refers to the theory that the behaviour of a system is the sum of the behaviour of its smaller and simpler constituent parts. Reductionism is reflected in the propensity of organisations, including governments, to break down large problems into smaller problems so that aspects of national security, for example, are dealt with separately by the ministries of defence, home affairs and foreign affairs. But this approach is inadequate for dealing with complex — or *wicked* — problems like terrorism or climate change, which require collaboration across bureaucratic silos because the resources and expertise for dealing with them reside in more than one agency.

[6] Karl Marx, *Grundrisse* (London: Penguin, 1973).

[7] Alvin Toffler, *Future Shock* (New York: Amereon, 1970).

run the risk of solidifying into a dogmatic and unthinking adherence to "templates". At the same time, the policy solutions — such as state-led industrialisation under the Winsemius Plan — that worked very well for one phase of Singapore's development, arguably locked us into a certain path with comparative under-development of our local small and medium enterprises and entrepreneurial ecosystem. Similarly, the better the government got at service delivery, the more the relationship between the government and the people became a transactional one, and perhaps even resulting in a sense of entitlement and learned helplessness.

More often than not, we make decisions in the expectation that the future will unfold in a certain way, based on assumptions that we hold today. We may not even be conscious of these assumptions, or realise how they shape our decisions. But such assumptions, even if they were valid in the beginning, are likely to become invalid in the future because of changes in our operating environment. It is only when we muster the courage to question these assumptions, and are prepared to jettison them, that we can then change, and influence the change — just as Raffles did in 1819, and the founding fathers of sovereign Singapore did in 1965.

Other countries, even small ones like Estonia and Luxembourg, show that it is possible to overcome their constraints and shape their own futures in bold and imaginative ways. In whatever way Singapore seeks to shape its own future, our attitude towards uncertainty will be key. It was Charles Darwin who recognised that uncertainty is a necessary pre-condition for change and adaptation to occur. How prepared are we to tolerate a certain amount of messiness that is essential for innovation and serendipitous change? Indeed, Singapore's history offers examples of how we can shape the world that we inhabit — the founding of modern Singapore in 1819 was an attempt to shape the geo-political environment in Asia in order to realise Sir Stamford Raffles' vision. Singapore's story, post-1965, is familiar to us; our founding fathers charted unconventional paths, often as acts of faith — tempered with pragmatism — to prove that the idea of sovereign Singapore could prevail. It was never blind hope.

These issues form the substrate of the four lectures that I delivered in April and May 2017 as the S R Nathan Fellow for the Study of Singapore 2016/2017.

In the pre-lecture interview, I was asked what I hoped the audience would take away from the lectures. This is what I said:

- First, that they will understand that our environment is a fast-changing and complex one.
- Second, that there are no easy answers; it is very easy to criticise from the side, but it is not easy at all to find the right answers.
- Third, that every major decision and every major policy is not an exercise in finding the absolute right answer. Instead, it is always an exercise in making the right judgment — not a hard right or hard wrong — but a balanced one that serves the best interests of the majority and the country as a whole.
- Fourth, you cannot make everybody happy. Also, judgments always have to be revisited now and then; what seems to be sensible now, may in a few years' time no longer be sensible. You have to be prepared to constantly change.

Despite black swans, unknown unknowns, uncertainties, accelerating change, and there being no *ex ante* right answers, there is reason to be hopeful and optimistic. We should feel confident that despite the challenges, particularly as a small city state, we have what it takes to successfully bring Singapore to SG100 and well beyond.

It is my hope that these lectures presented some of the challenges and actions of the Singapore government in a fresh light, with new insights; that they demonstrated how we are now at the leading edge of governance; and that there is a basis for confidence in the future — provided we are prepared to embrace change and act on it.

There are many people whom I would like to thank. First, all of the donors who made this Fellowship possible. Second, IPS for thinking of inviting me and for supporting these lectures and their publication. Third, Devan Janadas for twisting my arm — very hard — to take up the Fellowship. Fourth, my friends and colleagues inside and outside government who helped me with research and ideas, including but not exclusively, Itzik Ben-Israel, Boey Yi Heen, Chen Jia'en, Hannah Chia, Chian Qing Ying, Benjamin Choy, Hannah Goh, Yulia Hartono, Adrian Kuah, Jeanette Kwek, Jody Lau,

Lee Chor Pharn, Lee Tzu Yang, Galen Lim, Aaron Maniam, Joan Moh, Dick O'Neill, Ashley Poh, Jared Poon, Terence Poon, Peter Schwartz, Ariel Tan, Liana Tang, Teo Yi Heng, Linton Wells, and Zhou Gangwei. Fifth, the four moderators of these lectures: Debra Soon, Chan Heng Chee, Chng Kai Fong, and Chua Mui Hoong, who all resisted the temptation to give me a hard time. Sixth, Fern Yu, my able and dedicated Research Assistant from IPS, without whose dedication and hard work this endeavour would not have been possible. Finally, I would like to acknowledge with gratitude the late Mr S R Nathan, a mentor for both myself and many other public servants, after whom this Fellowship is named.

ABOUT THE MODERATORS

Chan Heng Chee is Ambassador-at-Large at the Ministry of Foreign Affairs of Singapore, and Chairman of the Lee Kuan Yew Centre for Innovative Cities at the Singapore University of Technology and Design. She is also Chairman of the National Arts Council, a Member of the Presidential Council for Minority Rights, a Member of the Constitutional Commission 2016, and Deputy Chairman of the Social Science Research Council.

Chng Kai Fong is Principal Private Secretary to the Prime Minister of Singapore. He has been a civil servant for 15 years.*

Chua Mui Hoong is Opinion Editor of *The Straits Times*. She works with writers in the paper and a network of contributors in Singapore and around the world to produce commentaries for the newspaper's Opinion pages. She also writes extensively on politics and public policy issues. She is the author of two books and co-author of a third, *Hard Truths to Keep Singapore Going* which is based on interviews with the late Minister Mentor Lee Kuan Yew.

---

* Mr Chng has since been appointed Managing Director of the Singapore Economic Development Board, with effect from 1 October 2017.

Debra Soon is Chief Customer Officer, and Head of English Audience Segment, at Mediacorp Pte Ltd. She is also Treasurer of the Singapore Committee for UN Women, and Chairperson of the Youth Sub-Committee.

Lecture I

HUNTING BLACK SWANS
AND TAMING BLACK ELEPHANTS:
GOVERNANCE IN A COMPLEX WORLD

Introduction

Before we begin, I would like to say a few words on the late Mr S R Nathan, after whom this Fellowship is named.

Mr Nathan had a long — and storied — career in public service. He started out as a social worker. He played an instrumental role in the founding of the National Trades Union Congress, and helped to lay the foundations of the Ministry of Foreign Affairs. As Director of the Security and Intelligence Division, Mr Nathan put his life on the line, without hesitation, during the 1974 Laju Ferry Hijack. Eventually, he became Singapore's longest-serving President, a position that he held with grace and distinction, epitomising the ideals of public service.

Mr Nathan inspired and trained generations of public servants like me in the craft of government. He brought to his work a broad-minded and earthy understanding of human nature and society. He avoided easy answers to the challenges of governance.

In the book, *S R Nathan in Conversation*, Mr Nathan was quoted as saying:

Policy decisions are complex — the straightforward "yes" or "no" an-swers often demanded by the critics are rarely possible. There are often

grey areas, compromises — there is never an ideal solution to anything.
You can very rarely have changes without some kind of sacrifice.[1]

This observation naturally brings me to the topic of this evening's lecture — "Hunting Black Swans and Taming Black Elephants: Governance in a Complex World".

This is the first of four lectures — and they are all connected — so this is therefore a bit of a scene-setter. But all these lectures are linked, and I shall use the framework of *complexity* to explain some emerging concepts of governance in each of the four lectures.

In addition, I shall use the approach of "circling and deepening", a description that has been applied to the late Nobel Laureate Derek Walcott's work. I shall revisit themes and examples in every lecture — circling and deepening around them — in order to generate new insights and fresh learning points.

But it is in this first lecture that I shall dive more deeply into complexity in order to explain what it is, and why it is so relevant to governments and to good governance in today's unpredictable and uncertain world. I shall also explain why the nature of governance is changing in response to complexity, and how governments can adapt to these changes.

Complexity

Stephen Hawking, the world-famous theoretical physicist, said, "I think the [21st] century will be the century of complexity."[2]

But what is *complexity*? And what is its relevance to governance?

Complex is different from *complicated*. An engineering system is merely *complicated*. It could be an A380 or a telecommunications satellite. Its inner workings may be very difficult for a layman, who is more likely than not to describe it as *complex*, when it is actually just *complicated*. Complicated systems have Newtonian characteristics in that they perform pre-determined functions that are predictable and repeatable, in which input leads to a predictable outcome.

---

[1] S R Nathan and Timothy Auger, *S R Nathan in Conversation* (Singapore: Editions Didier Millet, 2015), 176.
[2] Glenda Chui, "Unified Theory is Getting Closer, Hawking Predicts," *San Jose Mercury News*, 23 January 2000.

In contrast, a *complex* system will not necessarily behave in a repeatable and pre-determined manner. This is because a system that is complex contains a large number of autonomous parts — agents connected to one another and interacting in a great many ways. They often generate their own feedback loops.

To understand the behaviour of a complex system, we must understand not only the behaviour of each of these agents but also how they interact with one another, and then how they act together as a whole. But with the current state of science, this is an almost insurmountable challenge.

Cities, like Singapore, are undoubtedly complex systems. They are made up of hundreds of thousands, even millions, of people, who are the *agents* in the parlance of complexity. Each person interacts with others, producing outcomes that often confound and astonish planners and policy-makers. Jane Jacobs, an American scholar of urban systems, aptly described the complexity of cities in her highly influential book *The Death and Life of Great American Cities*. She wrote:

> City processes in real life are too complex to be routine, too particularized for application as abstractions. They are always made up of interactions among unique combinations of particulars, and there is no substitute for knowing the particulars.[3]

All human systems are complex, not just cities. Countries are complex, as are political systems. The world as a whole is complex.

There are many definitions of complexity, but all of them agree that complex systems are characterised by the property of *emergence*. The connections and interactions among the many agents in a complex system lead to outcomes that are inherently unpredictable *ex ante*, and that are only revealed when they actually occur. So, when something happens, we are surprised.

Black Swans

Nassim Nicholas Taleb famously described one class of such surprises — rare and hard-to-predict events — as *black swans*.[4]

---

[3] Jane Jacobs, *The Life and Death of Great American Cities* (New York: Random House, 1961), 441.
[4] Nassim Nicholas Taleb, *The Black Swan: The Impact of the Highly Improbable* (New York: Random House, 2007).

In Taleb's view, black swans are not just surprising, but also have another important characteristic: their impact is large and game-changing.

In 2002, not long after 9/11, Donald Rumsfeld who was then US Secretary of Defense, introduced us to a close relative of the black swan, the *unknown unknown*. He said:

> *There are known knowns. These are things we know we know. We also know there are known unknowns. That is to say we know that there are some things we do not know. But there are also unknown unknowns, the ones we don't know we don't know.*[5]

Now, you may laugh, but if you are in the business of government, or if you have at least a passing interest in our future, then you ought to understand what *known unknowns* are, and what *unknown unknowns* are, because you are going to be surprised by both every now and then. And it helps to understand the difference between them.

Strategic Surprise

As a young officer in the Ministry of Defence (MINDEF) in the early 1980s, I think I would have found it very difficult, if not impossible, to grasp the concept of transnational terrorism that today preoccupies governments around the world, because the conditions that produced Al-Qaeda and the Islamic State did not exist in those days. And in those days, cyber warfare was a concept that we could only dimly understand because the underlying technology was only just emerging. Today, such things have become part of mainstream thinking.

Indeed, one of the foremost challenges facing any government is the challenge of strategic surprise.

Singapore has experienced many of our own strategic surprises in our short life as an independent state. The Asian Financial Crisis of 1997/1998 was one, as was the uncovering of the Jemaah Islamiyah (JI) terrorist network in December 2001. The Severe Acute Respiratory Syndrome (SARS), which hit Singapore in February 2003, precipitated a national crisis, leaving

---

[5] Donald H. Rumsfeld, "Department of Defense News Briefing," 12 February 2002, http://archive.defense.gov/Transcripts/Transcript.aspx?TranscriptID=2636.

more than 30 people dead, and caused a recession that year. From 2008 to 2009, the shocking and unexpected collapse of Lehman Brothers led to the global economic and financial crisis. Since then, there has been a succession of shocks, including the drastic plunge in oil prices that began in 2014, the reverberations of which are still being felt today, Brexit, and most recently, the US Presidential Election.

The Butterfly Effect

The complexity of our world owes a lot to its highly interconnected nature. The world has been transformed by huge leaps forward in technology in the last half century, especially in telecommunications and more recently the Internet. These, combined with innovations in transportation such as the container and commercial jet aircraft, have catalysed globalisation and led to vastly increased trade as well as the movement of people around the world. The resulting increase in density of connections and feedback loops has in turn greatly increased complexity at the global level.

In this highly interconnected world, what happens in one part is going to affect other parts — the so-called *butterfly effect* which postulates that the flap of a butterfly's wings in Brazil can set off a tornado in Texas. This was the title of a lecture by Dr Edward Lorenz. The butterfly effect is the concept that small changes in initial conditions can produce large effects in a complex system.[6] Not surprisingly, it was in weather forecasting that scientists gained a lot of insights into this phenomenon. More generally, events and actions in different parts of a highly interconnected system interact with one another in complex, non-linear ways, to produce effects that are difficult to determine *ex ante*. Instead, to use the term I introduced earlier, their behaviour is *emergent*. To reiterate, this is the defining characteristic of the complex world that we live in today.

The Tohoku Earthquake

A vivid example of the butterfly effect is the Tohoku earthquake that occurred six years ago. Japan is one of the most seismically active regions

---

[6] Edward Lorenz, "Does the Flap of a Butterfly's Wings in Brazil Set Off a Tornado in Texas?" (presentation, Global Atmospheric Meeting 139th Meeting of the American Association for the Advancement of Science, Washington DC, 29 December 1972).

in the world. So why was the calamity that befell Japan on 11 March 2011 such a big surprise? Was it because of the scale of the disaster? Indeed, the Tohoku earthquake and tsunami were a huge catastrophe for Japan. It killed around 18,000 people and resulted in direct material damages estimated by some at well over US$250 billion for Japan, making it the most expensive natural disaster in history.

But an equally important reason is the butterfly effect — the chain of events, beginning with the earthquake, which triggered a large tsunami, which then damaged the Fukushima nuclear power plant, causing a meltdown and radiation leakage. Arguably, it was the meltdown that was the *black swan*. Its impact was felt far beyond Japan, like the hypothetical tornado in Texas. It brought the safety of civilian nuclear power into question, not just in Japan, but around the world, and led one major economy half a world away from Fukushima — Germany — to forswear its use.

The Fukushima nuclear disaster was the result of complex interconnections and interdependencies, combined in this case with significant human failures including outright negligence and what Margaret Heffernan called "wilful blindness" in her book of that title.[7] The reality is that it is extremely difficult to estimate the cumulative effects of such complex events. It makes preparing for unforeseen situations an exercise fraught with difficulty. It also adds to the challenges of governments operating in complex situations.

The Arab Spring

In December 2010, Mohamed Bouazizi, a street vendor in Tunis, set himself alight. He was upset over harassment by the authorities. It was a *terminal* protest, because he died from the self-immolation. But that single act — a single event — triggered the Arab Spring. The consequences were dramatic. Governments collapsed in Tunisia, Egypt, Libya and Yemen. Governments changed in Kuwait, Bahrain and Oman. A civil war broke out in Syria, and it is still raging more than six years after Bouazizi killed himself. It can be argued that these events set the stage for the rise of the Islamic State.

The most imaginative novelist could not have written the script for the Arab Spring. It would have taken the bravest analyst a huge leap of

---

[7] Margaret Heffernan, *Wilful Blindness: Why We Ignore the Obvious at our Peril* (New York: Simon and Schuster, 2011).

imagination to predict the Arab Spring, such as it was. Truth, as it is often said, is stranger than fiction.

The famous British historian and politician, H. A. L. Fisher, concluded in 1935, not without a touch of irony, that:

> *Men wiser and more learned than I have discerned in history a plot, a rhythm, a predetermined pattern. These harmonies are concealed from me. I can see only one emergency following another ... and only one safe rule for the historian: that he should recognise in the development of human destinies the play of the contingent and the unforeseen.*[8]

In other words, we shall continue to be surprised.

Hindsight

The Arab Spring has spawned a growth industry. There are now countless political and social scientists, historians and Arabists all trying to explain the causes of the Arab Spring. Many will find convincing reasons as to why these events unfolded as they did.

But all this will be in retrospect. It is in the very nature of such post-mortem analyses that thinking and explanation must be fundamentally backward-looking. That explanations *after the fact* are the norm for strategic surprises like the Arab Spring and the Fukushima nuclear disaster under-lines the lack of any simple patterns in the complex world in which we live.

The 19th century Danish philosopher, Søren Kierkegaard, observed that "life can only be understood backwards; but it must be lived forwards."[9] You can look backwards in time to understand why something happened. That is hindsight. But hindsight does not necessarily translate into foresight. Simply because we can provide an explanation for why the current state of affairs has arisen does not mean that we are in a position to forecast the next drama or political catastrophe. Instead, these outcomes seem to be lurking somewhere,

---

[8] H. A. L. Fisher, *A History of Europe* (London: Eyre and Spottiswoode, 1935).
[9] James Daniel Collins, *The Mind of Kierkegaard* (Princeton, NJ: Princeton University Press, 1953), 37.

hidden from view, just over the horizon or around the corner, to surprise us when we least expect it. That is the problem. We cannot predict the future.

Undoubtedly, there are fascinating "what if" questions arising from the drama of the Arab Spring. What if Mohamed Bouazizi had not set himself on fire? Or what if he had survived the self-immolation? Would there have been an Arab Spring?

The fact of the matter is that we cannot really answer such "what if" questions. The propensity to agonise over and analyse surprising and shocking events such as the Arab Spring satisfies the emotional need for answers to questions like *what if* and *why*. But such illumination will not necessarily help us to anticipate or avoid the next strategic shock. The future is neither inevitable nor immutable. Applying the lessons of history is not enough to guide us down the right path into the future. Indeed, it is doubtful whether a single right path even exists.

Singapore's founding Prime Minister, the late Mr Lee Kuan Yew, said in 1983:

> *The past 24 years were not pre-ordained. Nor is the future. There will be as many unexpected problems ahead, as there were in the past.*[10]

It sounds like a truism, but it is the reality that governments have to deal with.

Complexity and Governments

The complexity of the world is something that governments should not ignore. The rise of complexity will generate more uncertainty, and increase the frequency of black swans and other strategic surprises. In other words, complexity can cause big headaches for governments.

On the other hand, governments that make the effort to understand complexity, and then to learn to manage complexity, will gain a big competitive advantage. While they cannot avoid black swans altogether, they

---

[10] Lee Kuan Yew, "Speech by Prime Minister Lee Kuan Yew at his 60th Birthday," (speech, Mandarin Oriental Hotel, Singapore, 16 September 1983) http://www.nas.gov.sg/archivesonline/data/pdfdoc/lky19830916.pdf.

will be in a better position to subdue the impact of strategic surprise and reduce uncertainty. They will also be better placed to exploit opportunities ahead of the rest.

Professor Kees van der Heijden, the pioneer Dutch scenario planner, said:

> *There are winners because there is uncertainty. Without uncertainty, there can be no winners. Instead of seeing uncertainty as a problem, we should start viewing it as the basic source of our future success.*[11]

In fact, it was Charles Darwin who first recognised that uncertainty is a necessary pre-condition for change and adaptation to occur. And it is complexity that produces the uncertainty essential for innovation and serendipity.

In this regard, economists like Ricardo Hausmann and César Hidalgo argue that the most important predictor of growth is economic complexity, or the diversity of products that an economy possesses.[12] So, complexity has an upside as well, and I will touch on this in more detail in my third lecture.

Yet, governments often ignore the complexity of their operating environment. They typically deal with complexity as if it is amenable to simple and deterministic, even linear, policy prescriptions. In a sense, the crux of public policy has been to apply — if not impose — orderly solutions to the myriad of complex problems that afflict our societies, our politics and our lived everyday experiences, in largely vain attempts to make what is complex merely complicated. We see this in legal systems that are based on uniform punishments to complex and varied crimes, in public health enterprises that treat patients as largely homogeneous, and education systems and pedagogies that assume that all children develop uniformly, or ought to.

Human Nature

This phenomenon points to an additional layer to the challenge of complexity, and that is our own human nature.

---

[11]Kees van der Heijden, Bradfield, Ron, Burt, George, Cairns, George, and George Wright. *The Sixth Sense: Accelerating Organizational Learning with Scenarios* (West Sussex: John Wiley and Sons, 2002), 13.

[12]César A. Hidalgo and Ricardo Hausmann, "The Building Blocks of Economic Complexity," *Proceedings of the National Academy of Sciences* 106, no. 26 (2009): 10570–75.

All human beings, including the great and the good, are afflicted with cognitive biases, or more simply, blind spots.

Many disruptions — natural disasters, pandemics, even financial crises and political upheavals — do not fall into the category of black swans. Instead, more often than not, they are either *known knowns* or *known unknowns*. Once upon a time, all disasters — storms, floods, earthquakes, volcanic eruptions — arrived without warning. Today, modern science helps to forecast such cataclysms with increasing accuracy. Many of such disruptions can now even be assigned probabilities. This ought to lead governments to take precautionary measures. But often, they do not.

In his bestseller *Collapse*, scientist and polymath Jared Diamond alludes to the inability to read trends or to see behind the phenomenon of *creeping normality*.[13] Things get just a little bit worse each year than the year before, but not bad enough for anyone to notice. It is like the proverbial frog in boiling water.

Indeed, people often have a hard time properly ascertaining the present value of events that will take place in the future. This tendency to discount the future — to place less emphasis on future risks and contingencies, and instead to place more weight on present costs and benefits — is a common cognitive bias known as *hyperbolic discounting*.

Governments are particularly susceptible to the cognitive bias of hyperbolic discounting. The institutional position that political leaders occupy discourages them from spending time worrying about a problem that will, hopefully, disappear, or only occur after they leave office.

This begs the question of how viable a public policy enterprise is, if the boundary condition is the term of a particular government at worst, or the lifetime of the already-born citizen at best?

Related to this is the question of responsibility and trade-offs. For example, it can be argued that the current generation has a responsibility of stewardship of the future. However, in order to fulfil that duty, certain tough decisions have to be made and taken in the here and now. How much appetite is there really for such long-term thinking, in this society or in any society?

---

[13] Jared Diamond, *Collapse: How Societies Choose to Fail or Succeed* (New York: Viking, 2005).

At the risk of generalisation, many governments tend to focus on immediate problems and priorities related to the election cycle. They would rather defer expenditure on something that may or may not happen.

This is why, despite understanding the threat posed to future generations by global warming, many governments discount those effects and instead place greater emphasis on the current costs of mitigation and adaptation — leading to sub-optimal policies — if one takes the long view.

The Black Elephant

This leads me to another member of my menagerie, the *black elephant*. What is the black elephant? The black elephant is the evil spawn of our cognitive biases. It is a cross between a *black swan* and the proverbial *elephant in the room*. The black elephant is a problem that is actually visible to everyone, but no one wants to deal with it, and so they pretend it is not there. When it blows up as a problem, we all feign surprise and shock, behaving as if it were a black swan.

Last year, many of us would have been astonished to learn that the Treasury in the United Kingdom had made no contingency plans for Brexit, despite the fact that the polls showed that the outcome of the referendum would be a close call.[14] The British military — which I presume is like most armed forces and makes contingency plans at the drop of the hat — also reportedly did nothing. The UK government looked decidedly flat-footed the day after the referendum. Surely this is an example of a black elephant? In fact, the only institution that had a Plan B was the Bank of England. My surmise is that because the Governor is not British — Mark Carney is Canadian-Irish — he had no emotional skin in the game, and could take an objective, dispassionate look at the situation.

In 2013, a small Ebola outbreak in Guinea ballooned within a year into an international health emergency in August 2014. Over 10,000 people died, and the economic cost to the affected nations in West Africa is estimated in the billions of dollars. But it could have been nipped in the bud if appropriate actions had been taken at the start.

---

[14] Gemma Tetlow, "Treasury Made No Plans for Brexit, says New Head Tom Scholar," *Financial Times*, 7 July 2016, https://www.ft.com/content/f5797e2a-444d-11e6-b22f-79eb4891c97d?mhq5j=e3.

These examples illustrate the tendency of the human mind to underestimate or ignore both sudden crises, as well as slow burn issues. Often, through hesitation and until events reach crisis proportions, no one takes any action.

Unfortunately, the black elephant is not an endangered species in the wild jungles of government. At best, we can try to *cull* them, but they are a resilient lot because of our collective cognitive failures.

Governance in Complexity

So, what can governments do to improve the way they manage complexity, and at the same time mitigate the effects of the various cognitive biases that afflict them?

One of the pioneer members of the Singapore Cabinet, Mr S Rajaratnam, was a very forward-looking person with a strategic outlook. Way back in 1979, he said:

> *There are the practical men who maintain that such speculations [or thinking about the future] are a waste of time and they have no bearing at all on solutions to immediate day-to-day problems. This may have been so in earlier periods of history when changes were few and minute, and were spread over decades and centuries... [but] we are not only living in a world of accelerating changes but also of changes which are global in scope and which permeate almost all aspects of human activity... Since change is about the future, then only a future-oriented society can cope with the problems of the 21st century.*[15]

Mr Rajaratnam was talking about the operating environment of a globalised and complex world, in which the pace of change is accelerating. How do we cope with that? We must learn to think systematically about a future that is inherently Volatile, Uncertain, Complex and Ambiguous (VUCA).

But herein lies the conundrum that all governments face. How do you make plans and policies for the long term, knowing that changes in the

---

[15] S Rajaratnam, "Speech by Mr S Rajaratnam, Minister for Foreign Affairs," (speech, seminar by the Singapore Association for the Advancement of Science, Science Centre, Singapore, 20 December 1979), http://www.nas.gov.sg/archivesonline/data/pdfdoc/SR19791220s.pdf.

operating environment are likely to occur within a shorter time frame, and that they will inevitably impact or even negate these plans? When you launch any big capital or infrastructure programme, you make certain assumptions. But inevitably, there will be changes in technology, and disruptions to the strategic environment. How do you factor in these changes, many of which cannot be foreseen, into plans and policies that we would like to last for 10, 20 years, maybe even much longer?

Foresight or Futures Thinking

We can start by accepting that complexity creates uncertainty. Prediction is not possible. Indeed, if it was, many of us would be out of jobs. Instead, as Mr Rajaratnam argued, the right approach is an orientation towards thinking about the future in a systematic way.

Clearly, changes need to be made to the way governments organise themselves. Their toolbox must be enlarged. We can adopt methods and processes that help us to reduce the frequency of strategic surprise, and when the inevitable shock occurs, to reduce the amplitude or intensity of its impact. Some of us call this *foresight*, or *futures thinking*. It helps policy-makers in government devise strategies and formulate policies to maintain positive trajectories and shift negative ones into a more positive direction. The goal is to make better decisions today that can help shape the future, rather than to predict the future, which would be a futile exercise anyway.

Scenario Planning

There are foresight methodologies — ways to think about the future systematically, and ways to help overcome some of our latent biases and our inherent cognitive constraints. One of them is the famous *scenario planning* method, which was developed and pioneered by the oil giant, Shell. In fact, by using scenario planning, Shell famously avoided the impact of the oil shock from an Arab oil embargo imposed in 1973 after the Yom Kippur War.

In the late 1980s, the Singapore government began using Shell's scenario planning techniques, starting in MINDEF.

Today, scenario planning is a key part of the Singapore government's strategic planning process. Indeed, the government takes scenario planning very seriously.

National scenario planning exercises are run every few years, and are even incorporated into the annual budget cycle. The resultant scenarios are used by ministries and agencies as a base reference for their own strategic planning.

The first effort at scenario planning at the national level in 1997 produced two scenarios — *Hotel Singapore* and a *Home Divided* — whose impact was profound. But they were particularly important then because, among other things, they helped to widen the focus of the government lens from geo-political and geo-economic issues to cover issues of Singapore society like ageing and social capital, local and community identity, and new fault lines. They led to the establishment of the National Volunteerism and Philanthropy Centre, and the Elderly Division in the then Ministry for Community Development. Their influence echoes to this day.

Used intelligently, scenarios make people aware of problems, uncertainties, challenges and opportunities that such environments would present — opening up their imagination and initiating learning processes. An example outside of government is Action Plan Singapore,[16] a series of scenario planning exercises run by the Institute of Policy Studies (IPS) starting last year, covering skills, longevity and innovation.

The big benefit of scenario planning is that it helps to overcome our cognitive biases by surfacing hidden assumptions and challenging mental models. It helps planners and policy-makers move out of their comfort zones, begin to think the unthinkable, and more willingly explore fresh strategies. Scenario planning helps to inculcate an *anticipatory mindset* in planners and policy-makers so that they instinctively raise "what if" questions on the issues they deal with. It helps them to overcome their blind spots, and to confront or at least be aware of black elephants.

---

[16] Action Plan Singapore was a series of scenario planning exercises run by IPS answering the questions: "What will Singapore's socio-economic landscape be like in 2026? How will the three issues of longevity, innovation, and skills affect that future?" The exercise was conducted in August and September 2016, bringing together about 100 participants from different sectors. More information can be found on the IPS website: https://lkyspp.nus.edu.sg/ips/event/action-plan-singapore.

Horizon Scanning

Notwithstanding these enormous benefits, scenario planning also has some limitations. Scenario planning is not very useful in locating the black swans and unknown unknowns that are lurking over the horizon.

The Nobel economist and strategic thinker Thomas Schelling explained:

> *One thing a person cannot do, no matter how rigorous his analysis, or heroic his imagination, is to draw up a list of things that would never occur to him.*[17]

To address this deficiency, even if only partially, in Singapore we have adopted other tools as well. While scenario planning remains the base, a wider range of foresight tools for *horizon scanning* are now deployed. Horizon scanning tries to identify the big game-changers by looking for emerging issues and trends, and delving into them to see where the threats and opportunities are.

To support this effort, the Singapore government also developed a computer-based suite of tools called the Risk Assessment and Horizon Scanning system, or RAHS. It is actually a pioneering big data system that is used to search for weak signals that could evolve into sudden shocks, among other things.

Collectively, these tools help planners to uncover and discover some, but certainly not all, of the black swans and unknown unknowns out there.

Wicked Problems

The complexity of our operating environment that produces black swans also produces *wicked problems*. Design theorists Horst Rittel and Melvin Webber described *wicked problems* as complex, large and intractable, with no immediate or obvious solutions.[18] They have causes and influencing factors that are not easily determined *ex ante*. They hardly ever sit conveniently within

---

[17] Thomas Schelling, "The Role of War Games and Exercises," in *Managing Nuclear Operations*, ed. Ashton Burton Carter, et al. (Washington, DC: The Brookings Institution, 1987), 436.

[18] Horst W. J. Rittel and Melvin M. Webber, "Dilemmas in a General Theory of Planning." *Policy Sciences* 4, no. 2 (1973): 155–169.

the responsibility of a single agency. Worse, they have many stakeholders, each of which sees these problems from different perspectives, and who have divergent goals. This means there are no immediate or obvious solutions, because nobody can agree on what the problems are in the first place, never mind what the solutions should be.

It is not at all difficult to find wicked problems. They include the big challenges of our age, such as climate change, the environment, population, urbanisation, inequality, and so on. Most crises are wicked problems. There are many stakeholders, but they have competing perspectives, different opinions and divergent interests. Please one and you upset many others. Solve one problem and others will arise.

Terrorism is a particularly wicked problem. Some of you might be surprised by this assertion, because you would think that all of us want to get rid of terrorism, except of course the terrorists. But even if everyone agreed on how to distinguish terrorists from legitimate freedom fighters, and there was consensus that terrorism should be banished, it is not clear that any policy prescriptions would gain universal acceptance. If that were the case, terrorism would not be the persistent problem that it is today, and the Islamic State would not be such a serious threat.

The German sociologist Ulrich Beck once wrote that:

> *The world has become so complex that the idea of a power in which everything comes together and can be controlled in a centralised way is now erroneous.*[19]

It means that there is no single agency in government that is really equipped to deal with a wicked problem in its entirety. But, letting departments tackle different parts of a wicked problem on their own often leads to duplication or to waste and sub-optimal policies, and even to new wicked problems.

---

[19] Ulrich Beck, "Muslim Societies and the Western World Can No Longer Be Considered to Be Separate Entities," *Deutschland Journal*, 15 September 2009, https://en.qantara.de/content/ulrich-beck-muslim-societies-and-the-western-world-can-no-longer-be-considered-to-be.

The Dangers of Reductionism

Efforts to understand our complex world and to deal with wicked problems often rely on an assumption — that what is complex can be reduced to simpler subsets that are easier to evaluate, and that when re-aggregated, will produce results that approximate the real world.

This approach is *reductionism*. It is rooted in the belief that complex phenomena can be analysed in component and simpler parts. The assumption is that after these parts have been analysed separately, it is then possible to understand the properties of the whole in terms of the properties and the interactions of these components. This assumption informs much of the methodology of modern natural science. It led to the tendency to dissect the complex world into smaller and less complex parts, and to favour explanations framed at the lowest level of scale.

Arguably, in government, the assumption of *reductionism* results in a tendency to divide big problems into smaller pieces. It goes a long way to explain the proliferation of agencies and bureaucracies as standard response to emerging and wicked problems.

But despite the enormous importance of this approach, it gives the false impression that investigating the features of things at a holistic level is less informative than investigating the properties of the components.

The Nobel laureate and physicist Philip Anderson argued against reductionism in his 1972 paper "More is Different". He wrote:

> *The ability to reduce everything to simple fundamental laws does not imply the ability to start from those laws and reconstruct the universe. In fact, the more elementary particle physicists tell us about the nature of fundamental laws, the less relevance they seem to have to the very real problems of science, much less to those of society.*[20]

Indeed, outside the realm of science, reductionism has not been as effective in explaining phenomena in such areas as ecology and economics.

Conventional efforts to model complex systems — like the think tank Club of Rome's model of economic and population growth, published in

---

[20] Philip W. Anderson, "More is Different," *Science* 177, no. 4047 (1972): 393–396.

1972 in the seminal *Limits to Growth*[21] and which had a profound influence on the population policies of countries around the world, including Singapore — have often gotten it badly wrong because of the faults inherent in reductionism. They link parts of a complex system together, assuming that these parts interact with each other in a Newtonian fashion, with clear link between cause and effect. Unfortunately, we now realise that complex systems often defy such deterministic analysis.

Complexity science abjures reductionism for the study of how systems interact with other systems, how agents interact with other agents, and then how these lead to *emergent*, rather than causal, results. Complexity science tools include agent-based modelling, which examines how autonomous agents interact with one another and influence system behaviour. These tools, when applied to economics and to other areas like urban planning, provide fresh and useable insights that deterministic models have failed to produce. In Singapore, government agencies are beginning to use such tools to address complex problems in areas such as land transportation, health and housing.

Net Assessments

Another way to counter the problems inherent in the reductionist approach is for the planner and policy-maker to look at situations — in particular, wicked problems — more holistically. This is important because, as many have observed, in our complex world, "everything is connected to everything else." If we look at each issue from a narrow perspective, we will miss the wood for the trees.

At heart, this is also an argument in favour of enlarging our field of vision to see how economics, demographics, societal issues, issues of environment and of technology, interact with each other to produce the complexities of the operating environment — the same complexity that generates wicked problems, black swans and unknown unknowns. This is a more interdisciplinary and a counter-reductionist approach.

Given the complexity of our world, interdisciplinary collaboration is essential for solving the big challenges of today, in science and technology,

---

[21] Donella H. Meadows, Dennis L. Meadows, Jørgen Randers, and William W. Behrens III, *The Limits to Growth* (New York: Universe Books, 1972).

in the social sciences, in the economy, in urbanisation, and in the environment. Why not also in geo-politics, geo-strategy and geo-economics? It is not possible, for example, to separate the conduct of foreign policy from other large national interests like economics and trade. So, there has to be a lot of internal coordination, and sharing of information.

To this end, inter-agency cooperation requires good leadership to grow. This is, in part, reflected in Singapore's coordinating ministers, a position first established in 2003 with the appointment of the first-ever Coordinating Minister for Security and Defence. Now there are three coordinating ministers who cover the entire spectrum of government functions — namely, national security, economic and social policies, and infrastructure. The establishment of these three positions marks the transformation of the Singapore government from a traditional hierarchy into a new age system of government, characterised by a Whole-of-Government approach.

Whole-of-Government

This transformation is significant, because the *Whole-of-Government* approach is an important response to managing complexity and dealing with wicked problems. The natural but often inappropriate reductionist approach would be to break down a wicked problem into smaller parts, and then leave it to each agency to make its own decentralised and bounded decisions.

In contrast, an organisation that breaks down vertical silos encourages the spontaneous horizontal flow of information that will enlarge and enrich the worldview of all agencies. This in turn improves the chances that connections otherwise hidden by complexity, as well as emergent challenges and opportunities, are discovered early. It is an environment in which officers consider the spill-over effects of what they do and their impact on the policies and plans of other agencies. It is a mindset of willingly working together to achieve common national outcomes, instead of serving the particular interests of individual agencies.

Take once again terrorism as an example. No single ministry or government agency — neither MINDEF nor the Ministry of Home Affairs — has the full range of competencies or capabilities to deal with this threat on its own. Instead, the efforts of many agencies have to be coordinated and brought to bear on this problem in a Whole-of-Government approach. This insight — and the looming challenge of transnational terrorism — led the Singapore government to set up the National Security and Coordination Secretariat.

Whole-of-Government looks eminently reasonable on paper. But while Whole-of-Government may be an imperative for dealing with wicked problems, it is not easily achieved. Governments, like any large hierarchy, are organised into vertical silos. For Whole-of-Government to work, these vertical silos need to be broken down, so that information can flow horizontally to reach other agencies.

But this is a Sisyphean effort. Whole-of-Government is antithetical to a deeply-ingrained bureaucratic instinct to operate within silos. More insidiously, institutional identity is sometimes so strong that it colours how each agency views or prioritises national interests.

Richard Nisbett, in his book *The Geography of Thought* takes this argument one step further.[22] He suggests cultural bias. For instance, Westerners tend to see the world in terms of individuals who are linked to others, and the surrounding environment, in axiomatic ways. From this emerges the emphasis placed in the West on individual rights and the rule of law. In contrast, East Asians — and here Nisbett refers primarily to the *Sinic* cultures — tend to see individuals, communities and their environments interacting more organically, in a dynamic ecosystem. Neither approach is more right than the other, but relying solely on either limits our ability to perceive problems from multiple angles.

Extrapolating from this, it is not hard to see why one of the big challenges of government — especially the hierarchical Westminster Western model from which the Singapore government is derived— is the occurrence of bureaucratic silos, where information and coordination flow vertically, rather than develop horizontally. This is, in turn, an organisational impediment to the sharing of insights and information critical to thinking about the future.

This is a big hurdle to overcome. It requires not just a lot of effort but also a real change of culture to surmount this instinct to operate within silos, in order to make Whole-of-Government work properly. Often, the

---

[22] Richard Nisbett, *The Geography of Thought: How Asians and Westerners Think Differently... and Why* (New York: Simon and Schuster, 2010).

leader must *nag* his people to remind them that the Whole-of-Government imperative takes precedence over narrow sectoral interests and perspectives.

But this mindset is so important to good governance in a complex operating environment that the Whole-of-Government approach is today a priority of the Singapore government. There are inter-agency platforms that have been established to share information among ministries, statutory boards and other agencies, in order to take in different ideas and insights, so that wicked problems can be viewed in their manifold dimensions. Coordinating bodies now deal with cross-agency strategic issues, like the National Climate Change Secretariat and the National Population and Talent Division. Two years ago, the government set up the PMO Strategy Group with the mission of Whole-of-Government policy development and coordination. And most recently, the government announced the establishment of the Smart Nation and Digital Government Group to give a further Whole-of-Government push to the Smart Nation effort.

Urban Planning

At this stage, let me take up the issue of urban planning, a uniquely wicked problem for Singapore. While other countries have large land areas, which allow new cities to develop and replace other cities that may decline in relevance and fortune, Singapore, as a small city state on an island, does not have that luxury.

Instead, urban planning in Singapore needs to take into account the challenge of packing in housing, green space, industrial land, commercial and retail space, land for transportation needs, and military training areas, all within the confines of a small island of 718 square kilometres. This is less than half the size of London, and only two-thirds the size of New York City.

In Singapore, the entire process of urban planning involves close collaboration among economic, social and development ministries and agencies. It also entails consultations with various stakeholders in the private sector and the general public. This Whole-of-Government approach enables all stakeholders to better understand interdependencies and implications of land use and strategic decisions.

Planning so far ahead and for multiple possible functions is inherently complex and invariably involves many uncertainties. So, national scenarios are used to factor in these uncertainties. Plans are also regularly reviewed. This process of long-term planning and regular review has enabled Singapore to anticipate its needs far in advance, and provides the flexibility to respond to surprises and to adapt to changes over time.

But such plans are only possible because of the embrace of a Whole-of-Government approach, in which trade-offs in land use are made among agencies. What is protected is not the narrow sectoral interests of the various ministries and agencies, but the larger national interest. It is not just a matter of coordination of roles and actions. At its core, Whole-of-Government means finding consensus on strategic priorities. Consensus is made possible because processes like scenario planning help align the government agencies to the larger national interests.

Whole-of-Nation

But with increasing complexity, the role of the government transforms from being a direct service provider, and becomes more of what the Manhattan Institute for Policy Research describes as a "lever of public value inside the web of multi-organisational, multi-governmental and multi-sectoral relationships."[23] This is sometimes called *networked government*, which refers to the management of the webs of relationships within and surrounding government. It is not just about strengthening the formal and informal networks within government, but also those outside of government, both locally as well as internationally.

For instance, government social services rely on collaboration with non-profit and community-based organisations. Examples like this do not indicate a diminishing importance of the government's role. Instead, government may be understood as having multiplied its capabilities by extending its reach beyond its institutional boundaries.

A government that operates in a networked manner deploys mechanisms that promote reach within the whole nation. Tackling the Jemaah Islamiyah (JI) threat has been a wicked problem for Singapore. It is not just about removing the immediate threat that the JI posed to Singapore's security.

---

[23] William D. Eggers and Stephen Goldsmith, "Networked Government," *Government Executive* (June 2003), https://www.manhattan-institute.org/pdf/gov_exec_6-03.pdf.

It also requires engaging multiple stakeholders, including community groups like the religious teachers who started the Religious Rehabilitation Group. It means engaging the private sector to help develop protective systems, processes and security infrastructure. This approach clearly needs not just the many agencies of government coming together, but also bringing in the people and private sectors.

In a way, it is not just a Whole-of-Government approach, but also a *Whole-of-Nation* effort. This is because the JI poses a multi-dimensional threat that requires not only collaboration among security agencies, but also with social agencies that have oversight of issues affecting local communities. The Singapore approach is to fight the JI network with *Whole-of-Nation* networks. This is networked government in action.

This Whole-of-Nation approach continues today with the SGSecure initiative, which is specifically targeted at building community networks. The SGSecure national movement aims to "sensitise, train and mobilise the community" as part of its response in the face of national threats.

Another example of the Whole-of-Nation approach is Our Singapore Conversation, a year-long process involving more than 600 dialogue sessions and nearly 50,000 participants. This process surfaced fresh insights for government and for citizens, such as the desire for broader definitions of success or greater assurance about health care and retirement, that would otherwise have been much more difficult to obtain. It provided the basis for the government to update, revise and change policies in response to a changing environment.

Conclusion

The rise of complexity in the world today throws up enormous challenges for governments around the world. Black swans will confront them, and they will have to deal with wicked problems. Black elephants will be lurking in the background.

Foresight will help governments to better deal with complexity and its challenges. The concept of governance must also change, in tandem with rising expectations and a more educated and empowered citizenry. Government-by-Agency will evolve into Whole-of-Government, which in turn will embrace the broader Whole-of-Nation approach that includes business, civil society and the man in the street. Collectively, these multi-sectoral actors will change the concept of governance, even if they are not part of "government", traditionally defined. The future of governance in a world of complexity lies in such systems-level coordination.

But I should conclude by recounting Winston Churchill's astute advice on the essential quality of a good government leader:

> *It is the ability to foretell what is going to happen tomorrow, next week, next month, and next year. And to have the ability afterwards to explain why it didn't happen.*[24]

Thank you.

---

[24] Bill Adler, *The Churchill Wit* (New York: Coward-McCann, 1965), 4.

Question-and-Answer Session
Moderated by Ms Debra Soon

Debra Soon (DS): I understand that there are some people in another room.[25] Well, my name is Debra Soon and I work for MediaCorp.

I have not had the privilege of working directly for Mr Peter Ho, but I had the privilege to observe him when he was Chairman of the Pro-Enterprise Panel, on which I was a committee member, several years ago. And, in that capacity, I had insight into his devious, strategic mind, because I noticed how he could, with just one very penetrating question, cause various senior civil servants opposite him to shift rather uncomfortably in their seats.

So I took some mental notes on how he managed to do that. I also saw why Janadas said that he was a very sweet boy. I can believe that he was very sweet, because he managed to ask his question in a very polite and gentle, and maybe perhaps, even sweet manner. I do not intend to cause Mr Ho to shift in his seat today, but perhaps you all might have some penetrating questions for him.

I will ask one question before I open it up to the floor. Mr Ho, you talked earlier about the proverbial frog in boiling water, and the dangers of creeping normality. What is the one issue in Singapore today, which you observed in your time in the civil service, that could have been a victim of creeping normality, and hence, could have been prevented, but which we are now still reeling from, or dealing with the consequences of?

Peter Ho (PH): Well, there are probably many issues of this nature, and I do not think there is a single issue that springs to mind as prominent or most impactful. But let us just think about the issues that we have had to deal with. One of them I would say is climate change — a classic example of how we failed to read the initial warning signs that it was a problem.

If you remember, things came to a head when we had this occurrence of flash floods, including at Orchard Road. Then we started to learn about terms like "ponding", and people also blamed dirty drains and clogged up canals for the floods. But when this problem persisted — and the floods did not just occur in Orchard Road but instead popped up everywhere — we realised that there was something more than dirty drains. To the credit of the Singapore government, it started looking at what was causing this flooding problem. What they realised was that, apart from the obvious contribution that is urbanisation, which creates a lot more challenges for drainage, the real problem was the intensity of rainfall had increased tremendously.

And what caused the increase in intensity of rainfall? It was rising temperatures! We live in a part of the world where rain is caused by convection. The rain becomes more intense when temperatures are higher. Even when you have a first-world, first-class drainage system — as we do, it is not good enough to cope with something as fundamental as rising temperatures, because the system is not scaled and designed for that. So every now and then, we are going to be confronted by these kinds of problems.

The key question is how long we take to respond. Usually, in Singapore, the government deserves quite a lot of credit for coming to terms with the reality, rather than let the system just stew, then blow up into a crisis. But just think of the drainage problem. We are now spending billions of dollars to revamp the entire drainage system, because it is such a big system. We are going to face more and more of these things, and if you attend my next lecture, you will understand why change is happening so fast that we can hardly keep up with it.

DS: What is one way to prevent, or at least, to reduce the time taken to come to terms with this sort of challenges?

PH: I will touch on this issue in a future lecture. But let me say that we actually need to have a group of people whose job is to just focus on these kinds of issues, because if you are just dealing with the day-to-day problems, you do not actually have enough bandwidth left to think about longer-term issues. And if you try to think about longer-term issues, it begins to impact on your own thinking and your ability to deal with the day-to-day problems.

So, you should have a group of people whose business is to just think about these issues and say, "What are the next emerging issues that are just lurking over the horizon? Are there any black elephants?" Sometimes, there are a lot of black elephants, but the question is, are you going to do anything about it? Sometimes you need a group, you know, like that little truth-telling boy from *The Emperor's New Clothes*, to point out the obvious, which everybody is pretending they do not see. The question is whether we are prepared to invest in this sort of capability.

The Singapore government has invested in it through the national scenario planning process, but also, more recently, by setting up something called the Centre for Strategic Futures. In fact, to my knowledge, we are probably the only government in the world that takes futures thinking as seriously as we do, and that thinks about the future as systematically as we do. I am not saying that we are perfect. We have not reached the tenth level of Nirvana, but I think we are doing relatively better than most.

DS: Thank you very much. Before I open the floor, for the people in the other room with questions, all you need to do is to write your question down and hand them to the staff, and they will bring them over.

Participant: You have taken us through the limitations of reductionist thinking, especially with regard to wicked and complex problems. What are the implications for the way that we train in school, or rather, train for the public service, and organise for it? Are specific disciplines still important, or would you then say that the way we educate public servants, or even think tankers, would be to send them to liberal arts colleges, for instance?

The second question has to do with reward. If you build up the ability to foretell the future, you want to get to a point where you can explain why something did not happen. How do you reward the success of dodging the bullet, of being able to say, "Well, look, this did not happen"?

PH: First, on the business of training. We have to be quite realistic that you cannot train everybody to be a futurist. It will be a disaster for any government — any organisation — to just have people who think about the future without worrying about the here and now, about how to bring home the bacon. So, we cannot do that.

But the people whom you are looking for are people who are very broad-minded. In my experience, those who do this kind of work should not stay too long in the business, because otherwise, they will also become victims of "establishment capture". They will be captured by a certain way of thinking, and the freshness is lost. Instead, you should always be looking for people who have breadth, not necessarily depth. And they must be open-minded and able to think for themselves.

Having said that, since you mentioned our education system, I think that increasingly the real problems of the world require an inter-disciplinary approach. They cannot be solved just by applying an engineering solution, and then you think you have solved it. In fact, many of the most difficult problems are going to be a combination of finding the technical solutions — which are in some ways almost the easiest solutions to find — and then combining them with the social insights or behavioural nudges to encourage people to use those solutions. In the future, a lot of emphasis in our educational systems will have to be placed on inter-disciplinary training.

If you think about the SUTD, the Singapore University of Technology and Design, it is probably one of the few institutions in the world, and certainly the first in Singapore, for which the inter-disciplinary approach is at the core of its educational philosophy. You have to do a lot more of that, because of the nature of the world we live in.

The second point about reward, you know, if you work in any organisation, you generally do not get rewarded for getting things right. But if you get things wrong, you will be scolded. The only appeal I would make is that the bosses need to be a bit more tolerant. But please do not start thinking that this is all about prediction and getting things right. When I quoted Winston Churchill at the end of the lecture, it was not without a touch of irony. Because the reality is, you will not always get it right. I am advising the Centre for Strategic Futures, and I do tell the staff there: you must have no ego in this business. You cannot have an ego because if you get it right, you will get no credit for it. And of course, if you get it wrong, you will be pooh-poohed and denigrated.

Participant: In terms of the global monetary economy, you have the International Monetary Fund, the World Bank and other organisations trying to solve the wicked problems of development and financial crisis.

But as we can see from the Asian Financial Crisis and the Global Economic Crisis, these black swan problems were not anticipated and were not solved quickly. That may have led to the development of regionalisation. Do you think that this is a good way to solve the world's problems — in this case, monetary problems — and what role can Asia, particularly Singapore, play in these increasingly multilateral approaches?

PH: Well, first, I am not an expert on all these international multilateral structures. But my observation is that we have shifted from a bipolar world, which was the world defined by the Cold War, to a world which one could argue was unipolar for a very short period of time, into something far more complex and messier. The changes that are happening today are happening in a way that is very hard to know where they are leading. In fact, the fundamental question we should ask ourselves is whether the changes we are seeing today are not just challenges for regions like Europe and in the United States, but more broadly, a pushback against free trade and the institutions that promote globalisation.

Whether this is just a temporary phenomenon, or whether in fact we have entered a new era, we do not know. Is this just a phase which, maybe four, five years down the road when things have settled down, people will come to their senses, and then things will be better? Or have we actually entered a new and far more complex phase? The world we know is actually a world defined after the Second World War by the victors. It is a world we have gotten used to living in, but does this mean that the world is basically on that trajectory, and we are just seeing some ripples around that general trajectory? Or is it something else? Has a basic change taken place? We do not know.

But we can already see some warning signs that this is more than just a passing phase, because we have got big problems in Europe. There is rising nationalism, there is increasing populism, and there is pushback against free trade. A big country is now saying that it is going to bypass the World Trade Organization — what does that mean? I think you cannot say that multilateral institutions, which are being bypassed or are being ignored, or whose contributions are being slashed by huge percentage as in the case of the United Nations (UN), are going to be in any position to restore the world to the status quo ante.

So, that is a long way of saying, actually, I do not know the answer to your question. But you have to start thinking through these things. And then you can, if you feel that it is just a passing phase, decide, okay, we just batten down the hatches and when the storm is over, things will be back to normal. That is one approach. But I suspect that is a bit of a "black elephant" approach. Instead, it could be a new phase, and if it is a new phase, you have to revisit every single policy, every single assumption.

DS: A participant from the other room asks whether, while the government embraces complexity, we think the public also needs to appreciate and understand the complexity of policy-making, and what goes behind government thinking?

PH: I think it is hard enough for the government to deal with complexity, to understand the meaning of complexity, and how it impacts on governance and the making of policy. It is going to be even more difficult for the public to understand complexity in the way I have presented it here. But it is not so much about complexity, because complexity is just a way of framing things. The basic point is that there are never easy answers. You can have a problem that arises in which everybody has different expectations of what the solution should be. It is the government's job to make the judgment over where the right median point is going to be. A lot of people will be unhappy, but it is the nature of government. It is their business. If you do not have the stomach for it, and you want to be popular all the time, you will be in trouble.

Participant: Given that the mainstream way of thinking is still largely Newtonian, and people — at least for me — still assume causality and have a simple cause-and-effect way of understanding the world, what are your insights on getting your message across to the public? Is this problem itself our wicked problem?

My second question is: What is the role of the traditional long-term way of thinking of causality in this new, increasingly complex world?

PH: Well, to your first point, it takes a certain specialised audience and discipline to talk about complexity. It is far more constructive to have dialogues to explain why problems are very complex, and why they are difficult and have no solution. But to try to get everybody to understand complexity is quite a different ball game. It took me years to understand complexity, and I do not even begin to think that I have anything more than a superficial understanding of it.

But I just wanted to make the point that Singapore's government is actually unusual. Today, complexity has crept into the vocabulary of civil servants. They use it a lot. Many of them do understand what it is. But some of them do not. The important point is that, at least the Singapore government has a fighting chance to deal with complexity and to manage complexity. I cannot think of any other government where you find an understanding of complexity in the way that I have framed it here. Here in Singapore, you can find it.

Which is why it is very difficult to think that global institutions can come together in a Whole-of-Globe, or Whole-of-World-Government way, to solve the world's wicked problems. It just cannot work. You look at the UN. It has got huge challenges just trying to get an agreement on some of those singular wicked problems, whether it is poverty or climate change, and so on.

On long-term thinking, there will always be a place in government for that. The question is, how do you think about the long term? Do you think about the long term as just a straight line to the future that you are able to predict, or do you think about the long term as perhaps something that is uncertain, where the future itself is indeterminate? This is a very critical issue because the environment we are living in is changing so fast. I will be talking about accelerating change in my next lecture, and this is one of the big problems!

Participant: In this complex world, most problems need long-term planning and strategies. On the other hand, politicians face short-term election pressures. Speaking about the hard truths is not always politically correct, and sometimes, almost like suicide. How do politicians make choices, and keep a balance?

PH: Well, every politician is caught on the horns of a dilemma. Many of the policies they want to make — for the best and most altruistic reasons — often require that they be in the position to see through these things over the election cycle. But they may have to make decisions that are so unpopular that they will not be elected to see through the implementation of these decisions. And if they are not going to be elected, a new party comes in, and new leadership comes in. All their great plans will come to nothing! This is in itself a wicked problem for a political leader.

I think in all these things, it is always about how you find the right balance. You know if you swing to one extreme, so that you just worry about your chances of being elected, then you will not do any long-term planning or thinking, and you will not plan for the future — you are not really helping the long-term interests of the people. On the other hand, if you just doggedly pursue a conviction that "this is the best for the long-term interests", then, in fact, you may not get the chance even to kick the ball down the road! That is the dilemma. And I see in some countries, the leadership are better able to find the right balance, in others, they are not. You can see the consequences when they do not find the right balance.

DS: Is it about planning for the long term, but communicating for the short term?

PH: Yes, something like that.

Participant: Mr Ho, you spoke on tackling wicked problems with a Whole-of-Government approach. You also mentioned a little bit about the UN, and how they seem to be falling short of solving world problems.

On the other hand, you have got organisations like the Bill and Melinda Gates Foundation — organisations from the private sector, which seem to be quite effective.

From a local perspective, maybe the government might acknowledge that they do not have a monopoly of all ideas. As we tackle Whole-of-Nation problems, what do you think of the private sector playing a much more central role, instead of being just members of an advisory committee or a government committee? Can the private sector take the lead? And government comes in, maybe to advise and share their insights. Do you see that happening in the future as we tackle more complex problems?

PH: There is certainly a very compelling argument for having both the private as well as the people sectors getting involved in governance, not just government. Government is an entity that obviously, by definition, excludes the private sector and the people sector. But governance, which is the government plus the people and the private sectors, clearly can do a lot more together. That is because the government today finds itself in a position where there are such complex problems that they have neither the monopoly of wisdom nor of insight. So I think you have to find a way to organise these relationships. It is not necessarily always going to be a comfortable relationship, but can they interact better? Can the private and people sectors take on more responsibility? Can they take on more work?

I think the answer is that they can, and they should, because in a complex world where nobody has a monopoly of wisdom, you want some additional insights. The question is, even if we say this is desirable and even if the government wants to do it, does the private sector want to do it? I am also of the view that, sometimes, when we talk about self-regulation, the private sector hates that! They dislike self-regulation because they have got no one to blame but themselves when something goes wrong! But the answer is yes, they should!

This is something that will evolve over time. You can see that steps have started to be taken in Singapore. On the economic front, we have been through all these economic review committees, which is a way of getting people from the private sector involved in issues of governance. Now, Our Singapore Conversation is a way of getting people involved on the social side of things, but it still has not yet reached the point that is sustainable. It is a work-in-progress. But, my own sense is that Singapore has moved further and faster down this road of governance than most governments.

Participant: I am a secondary school teacher, and I am keen to hear your thoughts on how we can get more teachers to understand the kinds of complexities that we are living with today, and how we would be able to help our students understand complexity, or even inter-disciplinary approaches, given that they are still quite young and not so mature.

PH: One way is to take the "design approach". It looks at the problem from different points of view, especially from the point of view of the people who are most affected by the problem. This is inter-disciplinary because there is no single discipline that can produce all the answers to such complex and wicked problems.

This is the way you should do it in the schools, and I think this is also the way they do it at SUTD. They take real-world problems because it is real-world problems that require this design approach or inter-disciplinary approach. More and more real-world problems require people from different disciplines to come together. So you can throw a real-world problem at your students, and ask them to solve it. They will discover that just having the science may not be enough. They must understand the societal context. They may have to talk to different people to see how these problems affect them, to understand what the problem really is from their perspectives, and therefore, what the possible solutions are. And remember — there are no right or wrong answers. And that this is, again, the real world.

DS: Thank you very much. Ladies and gentlemen, on that note, let us thank Mr Ho for his time.

Lecture II

GOVERNING IN THE ANTHROPOCENE: RISK & RESILIENCE, IMAGINATION & INNOVATION

Introduction

This series of lectures touch on the challenges of governance in an era of growing complexity. But during Singapore's early years, our founding fathers were seized with multiple critical and urgent problems of the day. They grappled with poor living conditions, political and economic uncertainty, and racial and religious tensions. For instance, Tuan Haji Othman Wok was instrumental in pushing for multi-racial and religious harmony in Singapore.[1]

If he, and the rest of our founding fathers had not carried out their task as well as they did, we would not be here today — a peaceful and prosperous nation, invested with the privilege of thinking about and preparing for the future.

Welcome to the Anthropocene

We live in the Anthropocene. Preceding epochs, like the Holocene and the Pleistocene, more commonly called the Ice Age, were all periods in the Earth's long geological history that date back four and a half billion years.

---

[1] Tuan Haji Othman Wok, one of the founding fathers of Singapore, passed away on 17 April 2017. The memorial service for him was held on 19 April, the same day as Mr Ho's lecture. Mr Ho paid tribute to the late Tuan Haji Othman Wok at the start of his lecture.

Humans have only existed in the last 200,000 years or so, from some-time in the late Pleistocene. This is just a blink of an eye in geological terms.

A view that is gaining currency in the scientific world is that human activity has begun to have a significant impact on the geology and the eco-systems of our earth. This is now often referred to as the Anthropocene, and many date its origin to the Industrial Revolution.

But what does the Anthropocene have to do with governance?

The Great Acceleration

In the Anthropocene, human activity is the prime driver of change in the earth's eco-system. What is most striking is that since the 1950s, after the end of the Second World War, change caused by human activity actually started to accelerate. This phenomenon is sometimes called the Great Acceleration.[2] Changes are now taking place at a pace and on a global scale that is unprecedented in history. The evidence is made visible in a spectrum of global indicators, including greenhouse gas levels, ocean acidification, deforestation, and loss of biodiversity.

It is not difficult to understand why. Today, increasing urbanisation is driving up consumer demand. Globalisation has taken off because of airline travel, container shipping, telecommunications and the Internet. Tourism is booming, and even the number of McDonald's restaurants increasing. As a result, the global economy is expanding, and the demand for infrastructure is growing. These combine to create a spiralling demand for resources — food, water and energy — that is straining the earth's ecosystem. Climate change is one major consequence, but it is only one of many dangers that lie ahead as the Great Acceleration continues unabated.

Technology is a major factor in propelling the Great Acceleration. Moore's Law says that computing power doubles every two years. It is still holding more than 50 years after Gordon Moore, the co-founder of Intel, made the observation. But it is not just computing power that is growing at an exponential rate. In his latest book *Thank You for Being Late*, Tom Friedman presents

---

[2] Will Steffen, *et al.*, "Global Change and the Earth System: A Planet under Pressure," *Springer* (2003), http://www.igbp.net/download/18.56b5e28e137d8d8c09380001694/1376383141875/SpringerIGBP SynthesisSteffenetal2004_web.pdf.

evidence that other technologies are also changing at a similar breath-taking rate, and he writes of "simultaneous accelerations in technology, globalisation, and climate change, all interacting with one another."[3]

The Fourth Industrial Revolution

If the Anthropocene started with the Industrial Revolution, Klaus Schwab, the founder of the World Economic Forum, argues that there have actually been three industrial revolutions since the 18th century, and a fourth is upon us. He explains thus:

> The First Industrial Revolution used water and steam power to mechanise production. The Second used electric power to create mass production. The Third used electronics and information technology to automate production. Now a Fourth Industrial Revolution is building on the Third, the digital revolution that has been occurring since the middle of the last century. It is characterised by a fusion of technologies that is blurring the lines between the physical, digital, and biological spheres.[4]

But he goes further to argue that the Fourth Industrial Revolution has no historical precedent because:

> When compared with previous industrial revolutions, the Fourth is evolving at an exponential rather than a linear pace. Moreover, it is disrupting almost every industry in every country. And the breadth and depth of these changes herald the transformation of entire systems of production, management, and governance.[5]

---

[3] Thomas L. Friedman, *Thank You for being Late: An Optimist's Guide to Thriving in the Age of Accelerations* (New York: Farrar, Straus and Giroux, 2016), 12.

[4] Klaus Schwab, "The Fourth Industrial Revolution: What it Means, How to Respond," 14 January 2016. https://www.weforum.org/agenda/2016/01/the-fourth-industrial-revolution-what-it-means-and-how-to-respond/.

[5] Ibid.

Singapore and the Great Acceleration

Singapore has experienced its own version of the Great Acceleration. In less than half a century, we moved out of the Third World and entered the First World. Furthermore, by most indicators, we are now in the top rank of the First World. Life expectancy has shot up, from 65 years when we gained independence after Separation, to around 83 years today, an astonishing achievement given that it happened within less than two generations. No other country has achieved so much in so short a time.

But an implication of this remarkable transformation is that change in Singapore has not occurred at a sedate pace. Unlike most countries that have tracked a more gradual path to the top, change in Singapore during this period has the *lurch of an acceleration*, rather than the *gentle sensation of a velocity*.

Within less than two generations, societal demands have moved from the basic needs at the bottom of Maslow's hierarchy — such as food, shelter, water and security — towards the more complex psychic needs at the top of the hierarchy, such as self-esteem, self-actualisation and transcendence, which are needs that governments find very difficult to service.

One could argue that this is a happy problem to be tackling, instead of dealing with a hardscrabble existence as a Third World country. But acceleration gives little time for government and society to adapt. Decision cycles are compressed within shorter and shorter time frames. But it is a treadmill from which we cannot get off, unless we are prepared to give up the quality and way of life that we enjoy today.

Consequences of the Anthropocene for Governance

Among other things, the Great Acceleration increases the complexity of our world, a challenge that I discussed in my first lecture two weeks ago. As a result, the Anthropocene today is characterised by growing Volatility, Uncertainty, Complexity, and Ambiguity — or VUCA, leading to an increase in the frequency of black swans and unknown unknowns. In other words, we will face bigger shocks, more often, but with less time to discern causes and respond.

With increasing VUCA, governments face two particular challenges:

- The first challenge is how to deal with inevitable *disruptions* that are the effect of rapid change. New technologies can disrupt, massively. Such disruptions could be black swans, but mostly, and luckily, they are not. Instead they are disturbances to the normal flow of life — a terror attack, a cyber-hack, a new virus, a flood, civil unrest, economic turbulence, and so on. They have a disruptive effect because we live in a highly interconnected and complex world. As the Great Acceleration causes interconnections to intensify, the frequency of disruptions will increase and the amplitude of their impact will grow.
- The second challenge is how to *manage risk*, which is the effect of uncertainty, and in particular, how to manage its impact on national aims and objectives, plans and policies.

I will now deal with each of these challenges, and how governments respond.

Disruption Is a Certainty

If disruption is a constant in our VUCA world, then it behoves us to spend time thinking about how individuals, organisations, societies and countries can respond. The pre-emption and prevention of disruption, despite our best efforts, cannot be guaranteed. The name of the game is not imperviousness to disruption, but recovering, and even growing, after being disrupted. This is resilience.

Resilience

Judith Rodin, the President of the Rockefeller Foundation and who launched the *100 Resilient Cities*[6] initiative of which Singapore is a part, provides a good definition of *resilience*. She writes:

> *Resilience is the capacity of any entity — an individual, a community, an organisation, or a natural system — to prepare for disruptions,*

---

[6] The 100 Resilient Cities initiative, pioneered by the Rockefeller Foundation, is a non-profit organisation dedicated to helping cities around the world become more resilient to the economic, social, and physical challenges of the 21st century. Singapore was selected as one of the 100 urban pioneers to spread the resilience movement across the world.

to recover from shocks and stresses, and then to adapt and grow from a disruptive experience.[7]

The SARS Case Study

On 25 February 2003, the Severe Acute Respiratory Syndrome (SARS) virus entered Singapore through three women who had returned from Hong Kong with symptoms of atypical pneumonia. The virus then spread with frightening speed through the hospital system in Singapore. It confounded our medical authorities in the beginning. They did not know how the virus spread, and why it spread so aggressively. The fatality rate was shocking. By the time the SARS crisis was declared over in Singapore, 33 people had died out of the 238 infected.

SARS was not just a disruption — it was a big *black swan* for Singapore. It was also a very frightening time for Singaporeans. Then Prime Minister Goh Chok Tong described it as a "crisis of fear".[8] Overnight, visitor arrivals plunged and the entire tourism industry came to a grinding halt. SARS severely disrupted the Singapore economy, leading to a contraction during the second quarter of that year.

A Resilient Response to SARS

When the normal flow of life is disrupted, as was the case during the SARS crisis in Singapore, societies need resilience to cope. Singapore's response to SARS is well documented. One of the most critical early decisions was to designate SARS a national crisis, and not just a public health problem. This meant that all the resources of government — and in fact of the nation — could be harnessed in a *Whole-of-Nation* approach to tackle the *wicked problem* of SARS. The Singapore Armed Forces (SAF) put an entire Army division at the disposal of the health authorities. The Singapore Police Force did likewise. Within weeks, MINDEF's Defence Science & Technology Agency (DSTA) and DSO National Laboratories developed a contact tracing system, as well

---

[7] Judith Rodin, *The Resilience Dividend: Managing Disruption, Avoiding Disaster, and Growing Stronger in an Unpredictable World* (London: Profile Books, 2014), 3.

[8] Goh Chok Tong, "Transcript of Singapore Prime Minister Goh Chok Tong's Interview with Mr David Bottomley, Correspondent, BBC" (interview, The Istana, Singapore, 21 April 2003), http://www.nas.gov.sg/archivesonline/speeches/view-html?filename=2003042201.htm.

as the infrared fever screening system now adopted around the world. Such innovations epitomise resilience during a crisis.

Efficiency vs Resilience

But this could not have been achieved if the government had been organised with an obsessive focus on efficiency and optimisation. These are well and good if everything goes according to plan. But things rarely go as planned. Most times, we cannot predict when disruptions will occur. The ability to quickly and decisively respond to crises and disruptions helps to manage uncertainty arising from our VUCA world.

Nassim Nicholas Taleb, who first coined the term "black swan" as a metaphor for strategic shock, notes that when disruptions occur in overly optimised systems, "errors compound, multiply, swell, with an effect that only goes in one direction — the wrong direction."[9]

But, as Taleb notes, "Redundancy is ambiguous because it seems like a waste if nothing unusual happens. Except that something unusual happens — usually."[10]

So, to deal with disruptions, governments must go beyond a rigid and unthinking emphasis on efficiency. Lean systems that focus exclusively on efficiency are unlikely to have sufficient resources to deal with unexpected shocks and volatility. There should be some *fat* or contingency capacity in the system.

Futures Thinking

This is not an argument for establishing bloated and sluggish bureaucracies. Indeed, it is worth recalling that in 1966, Lee Kuan Yew said that, "Societies like ours have no fat to spare. They are either lean and healthy or they die."[11] That maxim rightly articulated and reinforced the scarcity-vulnerability narrative, which was appropriate for a time when

---

[9] Nassim Nicholas Taleb, *Antifragile: Things that Gain from Disorder*, Incerto series vol. 3 (New York: Random House, 2012), 324.

[10] Ibid., 69.

[11] Lee Kuan Yew, quoted in Chan Heng Chee, "The PAP and the Structuring of the Political System," in *Management of Success: The Moulding of Modern Singapore*, ed. Kernial Singh Sandhu and Paul Wheatley (Singapore: Institute of Southeast Asian Studies, 1989), 70.

Singapore was hardly in a position to be profligate in its spending. It reinforced the need to be prudent in the use of our resources, and to save what we could for a rainy day.

But one thing that governments ought to have — as indeed should any large organisation that is concerned with its survival over the long term — is a small but dedicated group of people to think about the future. Their job is to look for challenges and opportunities emerging over the horizon. This is why I spent a good portion of my first lecture on the importance of this capacity. In Singapore, the government set up its own think tank for foresight, the Centre for Strategic Futures.[12]

The skill-sets for thinking about the future, which is inherently uncertain and unpredictable, are quite different from those required to deal with short-term volatility and crisis. Also, those charged with thinking about the future should be allocated the bandwidth to focus on the long term, without getting bogged down in the *minutiae* of day-to-day routine.

Of course, one could argue that it is the business of all government agencies — and the government as a whole — to prepare for the future. But even if they try to do that, it is not always easy for the planner or policy-maker to challenge the *official future*, especially when that future is consistent with an organisation's biases and preconceptions. Those who articulate a radically different future are at danger of being branded as subversive or lacking a sense of reality. So they will have a real incentive to make their scenarios more palatable for their audiences. But in so doing, they also inadvertently reduce the impetus for the organisation to confront uncomfortable alternative futures and to prepare itself for them. That is why Peter Schwartz, one of the most important of Shell's scenario planners, once said those whose job is to think about the future should also be court jesters — who can say the most ridiculous things and get away with it. They are supposed to help us suspend our beliefs, and maybe our disbeliefs.

---

[12] The Centre for Strategic Futures is a futures think tank under the Prime Minister's Office. It was set up in 2009 with the mission of positioning the Singapore government to navigate the strategic challenges of the future and to harness potential opportunities. It does so by (a) building capacities, mindsets, expertise and tools for strategic anticipation and risk management; (b) developing insights into future trends, discontinuities and strategic surprises; and (c) communicating insights to decision-makers for informed policy planning.

Of course, this will not eliminate shocks. But by improving the ability to anticipate such shocks, we can reduce their frequency and impact. In turn, this will help make governments and nations more resilient.

Maintaining Reserves

Another part of the answer is the availability of reserves — if not reserves in natural resource, then other kinds of national reserves built from prudent policies and forward planning, or saving for the proverbial rainy day.

The SAF and its supporting organisations like DSTA and DSO are part of the reserves of the nation in the sense that they are an insurance policy, and a large one at that, for a contingency that will hopefully never occur. But without that *fat* in the system, it is doubtful that Singapore would have been able to respond to the SARS crisis as it did in 2003.

Singapore's government is also committed to building ample financial reserves from the savings and surpluses of the government budget, giving the country a buffer to draw on in times of crisis. This is a reason why Singapore has one of the largest reserves in the world, at least on a per capita basis.

The utility of the national reserves was evident during the 2007–2008 Global Financial Crisis. The Singapore government for the first time drew on the national reserves in the form of a S$20.5 billion Resilience Package. The name was not chosen randomly, I can assure you. This was primarily aimed at preserving and enhancing business competitiveness as well as promoting job retention, during a period of great uncertainty. A key aspect involved encouraging firms not to retrench workers, but to support retraining programmes, and to provide temporary part-time arrangements. Once the world economy began to recover, Singapore firms were able to respond with alacrity and speed to *catch the winds* of global economic recovery.

SkillsFuture is another example of how Singapore tries to *future-proof* the workforce by establishing a norm of lifelong learning, and by creating the infrastructure to make continuing education possible. Because it is not always possible to predict manpower trends accurately, having a system in place to encourage upgrading, and a culture that encourages lifelong learning, will help Singapore and Singaporeans ease through changes and uncertainties in the employment landscape. It is part of a larger effort to ensure that Singapore remains resilient in the face of uncertainty and future shock.

Trust

But another issue was at play during the SARS crisis: fear. It rears its head not only during deadly epidemics. Even in financial crises, as in 2008 after Lehman Brothers collapsed, fear can go viral. As Franklin Delano Roosevelt said during the Great Depression in 1933, "the only thing we have to fear is fear itself."[13]

The dissemination of trusted information is an important way of managing fear. During the SARS outbreak, Singapore took a transparent approach. The government laid bare the uncertainties and risks during SARS, even as other countries sought to reassure their citizens that SARS was under control. Singaporean leaders told people not only what they knew, but also what they did not know. They shared their concerns. They avoided providing false assurances.

This diffusion of trusted information — transparency, laying bare uncertainties and acting with empathy — was possible because of, and built on, the underlying trust, not just of the people in the government, but also of the government in the people. Singaporeans trusted the government for its effectiveness and integrity. The government trusted Singaporeans to deal maturely with the uncertainty as the SARS outbreak unfolded. This two-way trust, between the government and the people, formed a deep source of national resilience in Singapore during SARS. Indeed, trust is an important theme in my lecture tonight, and I will return to it later on.

Antifragility

Nassim Nicholas Taleb introduced another term, "antifragile", in his book of the same name.[14] His proposition is that if fragile things break when exposed

---

[13] Franklin D. Roosevelt, "Inaugural Address: Address by Franklin D. Roosevelt, 1933" (speech, Joint Congressional Committee on Inaugural Ceremonies, Washington, DC, United States, 4 March 1933), https://www.inaugural.senate.gov/about/past-inaugural-ceremonies/37th-inaugural-ceremonies/.
[14] Nassim Nicholas Taleb, *Antifragile*.

to stress, then something that is the opposite of fragile would not just hold together when put under pressure. Instead, it would actually get stronger. He calls this the quality of *antifragility*.

Strengthening the Social Fabric — Antifragility in Action

As I noted earlier in the definition by Judith Rodin, a resilient society not only returns to the state it was at before the disruption; it also adapts and grows. Similarly, an antifragile society reaches a new state, almost like a muscle that, tested by stress, grows stronger.

The cornerstone of Singapore's counter-terrorism strategy is a community response plan. This enhances community vigilance, community cohesion and community resilience. Singapore has built networks of community leaders and influencers by forming the Inter-Racial and Religious Confidence Circles (IRCCs). Through these networks, the leaders have helped strengthen understanding and build ties between different races and religions. For the Muslim leaders, they not only speak out against those who distort Islam, but also use the media, mosque and madrasah to assert mainstream Islamic values.

Singapore is also one of only six countries with structured programmes to rehabilitate and re-integrate terror detainees into society. The Religious Rehabilitation Group (RRG) was set up in 2003 after the Jemaah Islamiyah (JI) terror plots were thwarted. RRG counsellors, all of them trained religious scholars and teachers, have helped terror detainees understand how they had been misguided by radical ideologues. The counselling sessions also extend to the family members of detainees. Every released terror-related detainee in Singapore has undergone counselling as part of rehabilitation. Most have returned to their families, found jobs, and integrated back into Singapore society.

The RRG also builds social resilience through outreach. It organises conferences, dialogues and briefings to educate the community — including in the mainstream schools and *madrasahs* — about key Islamic concepts that have been misinterpreted and misrepresented by terrorist and extremist groups such as JI, Al-Qaeda and ISIS.

The example of the RRG illustrates a broader point. Just as trust between the government and citizens in Singapore predated SARS, strengthening the social fabric has been a key strategy since independence.

Singapore takes an interventionist approach to promote social mixing. It uses quotas to avoid the build-up of racial enclaves in public housing estates. It has introduced a raft of policies to ensure that growth is inclusive: investments in public education, grants for skills training, and tax credits for the working poor.

Strengthening the social fabric also means building antifragility through simulations, designed not just to hone citizens' and agencies' instincts of how to respond in crises, but also to build confidence that we *can* overcome crises. The most recent initiative in this vein is SGSecure.[15] In addition to raising awareness, SGSecure also runs exercises. This psychological strengthening is a key dimension of what Singapore calls Total Defence.[16]

Risk

Let me now turn to my second area of focus in this lecture: risk. Disruptions, such as a terrorist attack or the SARS epidemic, are examples of *risk events*, acute and discrete occurrences. A *risk issue* is a development or trend that evolves over time. For example, the rise of transnational terrorism is a risk issue.

Risks can be defined not just in terms of trends or events, but in terms of whom it affects. There are *enterprise risks* that have an effect on an agency's objectives. These include operational risks that arise from the agencies' day-to-day operations and services.

And there are the *strategic risks*. There will always be threats to national outcomes, policies and plans, because no amount of analysis and forward planning will eliminate the volatility and uncertainty that exist in a complex world. These threats constitute strategic risk.

By their very nature, strategic risks often arise out of wicked problems, and involve cross-cutting issues that require a focus on the inter-connections between risks. In other words, strategic risks need to be dealt with at a *Whole-of-Government* or even a *Whole-of-Nation* level.

---

[15] SGSecure is a national movement launched by the government in 2016 to sensitise, train, and mobilise Singaporeans to prevent terrorist attacks, through the three pillars of vigilance, cohesion, and resilience.

[16] Total Defence, launched by the government in 1984, is a concept that involves the participation of every Singaporean to deal with crises. It consists of five pillars: psychological defence, social defence, economic defence, civil defence, and military defence.

The Problem of Cognitive Dissonance

After the Asian Financial Crisis, in the boom years leading up to 2008, most people dismissed the risk of another financial crisis happening. Before 2008, central bankers felt that they had mastered macroeconomic management to the extent that prolonged inflation and deep recessions were no longer possible. A massive *hubris* dominated the financial world. Those who foresaw an impending crisis were roundly ignored. The consequence — the global financial and economic crisis of 2008/2009 — was catastrophic and tragic.

Much of our reluctance to grapple with game-changing issues such as the global financial and economic crisis stems from an unwillingness to face the consequences of an uncertain and unpredictable future. These consequences interfere with long-held mental models — and business or self-interest — creating *cognitive dissonance*. At the heart of it, cognitive dissonance is about denial: the inability to acknowledge uncertainty, and an unwillingness to accept the need to adapt to a future that might be radically different from the current reality.

Cognitive dissonance leads to many organisations, including govern- ments, underestimating risks, ignoring warning signs of impending crisis, and taking decisive action only when the crisis unfolds. This is the mother lode of *black elephants*, which I described in my first lecture. You can be sure that unlike its endangered real-life cousins, the black elephant is a species that is thriving in the Anthropocene.

How can we limit or counter the influence of such bias? Obviously, the occurrence of a crisis that radically alters our mental models is one corrective. The SARS crisis forced the Singapore government — as well as governments in China and Hong Kong — to take more deliberate steps to prepare for future pandemics. SARS corrected our biases, making us realise that the risks and costs of a pandemic were not trivial, and increased our alertness to the onset of another pandemic. Without SARS, it is difficult to imagine that our subsequent responses to the bird flu and the swine flu would be as aggressive and proactive as they have been. Contrast our response, and that of other Asian governments such as China and Hong Kong, with the lack of urgency in other countries which were largely unaffected by SARS.

But while crises can break our outdated mental models, they are an expensive way to force recognition of our biases. No government or society should have to wait for an actual terrorist attack to take the threat of terrorism seriously.

Risk as a Social Construct

Many big risks that governments have to deal with — natural disasters, pandemics, even financial crises and political upheavals — can often be assigned probabilities. This ought to lead governments to take precautionary measures to mitigate these risks. But often they do not, because of cognitive problems.

It seems to me that big risk is ultimately not the province of actuaries. Instead it is a broader social construct, meaning that an organisation and its people need to agree that a risk exists. This is important, as resources need to be allocated to prevent the risk, or to mitigate its impact, for example through contingency planning.

For obvious reasons, Japan takes the earthquake risk very seriously, because it is the most seismically active country in the world. Everyone in Japan understands that earthquakes pose a perennial and at least life-altering, if not existential, threat. Because there is a national consensus, no expense has been spared to make Japan resilient to earthquakes to the maximum extent possible.

But before Fukushima, there was no such consensus on nuclear safety. Most Japanese believed that nuclear power was safe because the authorities declared it to be safe. They were lulled into complacency by this rhetoric. It proved to be a dangerous assumption. So, the triple disaster of 2011 — the Tohoku earthquake, the tsunami that followed, and the Fukushima nuclear disaster — was accentuated, because nuclear accidents were not in the Japanese pantheon of serious risk. No doubt, the Japanese now take the risk of nuclear accidents much more seriously.

But it is not just natural catastrophes that are risks. One risk issue attracting a lot of attention these days is Artificial Intelligence (AI). A hypothesis gaining traction is that AI poses an existential risk — in the vivid imagination of some, perhaps of the Terminator Skynet kind — and that this risk is in need of much more attention than it currently commands. It is a view that has attracted the support of famous names like Elon Musk, Bill Gates and Stephen Hawking.

Of course, the cost of responding to some extreme risks can be too high, especially when governments are seen as spending inordinate resources to prepare for a host of eventualities that may never happen. For instance, there is a possibility of the earth being destroyed by a planet-killing aster-oid, but this is probably not a risk that we can meaningfully prepare for at this point in time, given the prohibitive costs today, that is, unless you are a Hollywood scriptwriter. We cannot eliminate every risk, but we need to manage them in such a way that strategies and their premiums do not have to be all front-loaded.

The reality is that agreement on what constitute the greatest risks to a nation must be reached through consensus. Without that consensus, the government and political leadership will find it difficult to allocate resource to mitigate these large risks. A national conversation to assess these risks is important. Otherwise, the alternative is to wait for disaster to strike before action is taken. By then of course it is too late.

Our Singapore Conversation[17] is an example of how risks are discussed at the national level. The risks of ill health emerged as a big concern during Our Singapore Conversation, and arguably gave impetus to changes in health policy such as the introduction of MediShield Life.

Risk as a Psychological Construct

Risk is also a psychological construct because people have blind spots, or cognitive biases.

For example, the *availability heuristic* is the tendency to overestimate the likelihood of events with greater "availability" in memory, which can be influenced by how recent the memories are or how unusual or emotionally charged they may be. So, after a terrorist attack, we will think that another terrorist attack is a more probable risk than something else, simply because it is fresh in our minds.

The availability heuristic is illustrated via an observation made by Gerd Gigerenzer, a German psychologist who studies risk. He found that in the months after 9/11, passenger miles on the main US airlines fell by between

---

[17] Our Singapore Conversation was a national conversation initiative that ran from 2012 to 2013. It involved more than 47,000 Singaporeans, in over 660 dialogue sessions across the island. The three main questions framing the conversation were:

1) What is the Singapore we want to see in the future?
2) What are our priorities, as a nation?
3) Where do we want to go as a country, as a people?

12 and 20 per cent, while road use jumped. The change is widely believed to have been caused by concerned passengers opting to drive rather than fly. But the reality is that travelling long distances by car is more dangerous than travelling the same distance by aeroplane. Professor Gigerenzer estimated that an extra 1,600 Americans died in car accidents in the year after the 9/11 attacks — indirect victims of the tragedy. [18]

Identification, management and communication of risk must take into account this human tendency to underestimate or overestimate risk because of their own cognitive biases or because it is inconvenient to admit to the obvious.

Risk and Uncertainty in Governance

It is inevitable that emerging technologies carry enormous risks, just as they promise huge opportunities. In recent years, a new wave of emerging technologies such as AI, drones, robotics, 3-D printing, big data, data analytics, cloud computing, and the Internet of Things (IoT), have begun to take off. Combined with the earlier wave of infocomm technologies, they promise to be disruptors and sometimes major game-changers, giving the individual capabilities and powers, which were previously the province of only governments and large organisations. Cities, societies and economies are becoming more and more disintermediated.

Arguably, such technologies and their applications have been an enormous force for good. And yet, governments do not fully embrace these technologies. At most they have reached a *wary* accommodation, exemplified in the Singapore government's decision to separate government computers from the Internet. And rightly so, because while these technologies bring undoubted benefits, they also create risks. There are pernicious uses of technology, such as in cyber-crime, and in the use of social media to promote extremist ideologies and to recruit terrorists. Social media also allows the proliferation of "fake news" that bedevils governments today.

Experimentation

In our VUCA world, there are no perfect answers in which outcomes are perfectly predictable. In such an operating environment, it is not always

---

[18] Gerd Gigerenzer, *Risk Savvy: How to Make Good Decisions* (London: Allen Lane, 2014), 9.

possible to make decisions on the basis of deterministic and linear analyses. Indeed, because change is happening so fast, such conventional approaches could lead us to miss the window of opportunity.

Instead, governments will often be called on to make big decisions under conditions of incomplete information and uncertain outcomes.

Of course, governments can play it safe and watch from the sidelines. But then, they will be overtaken by those who are nimbler, and those who are more daring. Or they can get some skin in the game now through research, test-bedding and pilots, so that they learn the limitations and potential of such technologies in order to be ready when these technologies take off. Pilot programmes and prototypes should be deployed where there is insufficient data for a proper analysis, or if there is no precedent to fall back on. Exploration and experimentation are often more valuable than predictions of analytical models. *Beta testing* can also encourage citizens to co-create by delivering potential value earlier, which in turn gets their buy-in.

Car-Free Sunday SG is an on-going initiative by the Urban Redevelopment Authority. Roads in the Central Business District (CBD) are closed on the last Sunday of every month. The rare opportunity and novelty of cycling or walking along the open roads of the city has attracted people in droves. Car-Free Sunday SG can be seen as beta-testing of a desired future state — a *car-lite* Singapore. The participation of so many people and the feedback that they provide are part of a co-creation process to determine Singapore's future land use and design.

But to experiment, governments must accept, and even embrace, certain levels of risk. It is a form of risk management. I call this approach *safe fail*, rather than *fail safe*. Fail safe means you risk nothing, but you also achieve nothing, and there is no progress. Whereas in a safe fail mode, if such experiments succeed, then they can be expanded. If they fail, then the damage is contained, and a lesson is learnt.

And of course, to learn from failure. Thomas Edison, the great inventor of the lightbulb, is also famous for saying, "I have not failed. I've just found 10,000 ways that won't work."[19]

---

[19] Nathan Furr, "How Failure Taught Edison to Repeatedly Innovate," 9 June 2011. https://www.forbes.com/sites/nathanfurr/2011/06/09/how-failure-taught-edison-to-repeatedly-innovate/#4d69ed9365e9.

The Innovator's Dilemma

The central thesis in Professor Clayton Christensen's seminal book, *The Innovator's Dilemma*, is that successful organisations are doomed to fail in the long run, because there is tremendous inertia to change a formula that has worked well. In other words, the incumbents of today are locked-in to their mental models and success formulas. They are prisoners of what they know they know. It is this inertia that allows the insurgents, the revolutionaries, the start-ups, to sneak in, change the rules of the game, capture market share and dislodge the incumbent.

While this conclusion is based on the study of companies, Professor Christensen told me some time ago that he thought the same principles apply to governments.

Clayton Christensen's solution to the innovator's dilemma is to create small self-contained units within the larger organisation that have the mandate to experiment with new ideas and new concepts. He writes:

> *The only instances in which mainstream firms establish a timely position in disruptive technologies were those in which the firm's managers set up an autonomous organisation charged with building a new and independent business around that disruptive technology.*[20]

If these new units succeed, then their formula can be proliferated through the organisation. If they fail, then the organisational impact will be contained.

A model of this approach is DARPA — the legendary Defense Advanced Research Projects Agency of the US Department of Defense that has been the force behind game-changing innovations like the Internet, GPS, and quantum computing.

In a similar though more modest vein, MINDEF set up the Future Systems Directorate (or FSD) — now known as the Future Systems & Technology Directorate — some 20 years ago with the mandate to think about the longer term challenges facing the SAF, and to come up with new operational concepts,

---

[20] Clayton M. Christensen, *The Innovator's Dilemma: When New Technologies Cause Great Firms to Fail* (Boston, Mass: Harvard Business School Press, 1997), xv.

experiment with these concepts, and then implement them. MINDEF knew then that the FSD would generate frictions and tensions in the system by the very nature of its mission. It would make many feel uncomfortable. But I believe that the FSD was the catalyst for the innovation and the spirit behind it that transformed the SAF from a Second-Generation into a Third-Generation SAF.

Going forward, this has to be the way for the SAF to stay ahead. It is not possible to maintain its strategic edge just by buying more and more weapons and platforms. The budget will not support this approach. Instead, the SAF's strategic advantage will be secured by exploiting its capacity to innovate and to change, changing the rules of the game, through better operational concepts and superior application of technology to realise these concepts.

Learning How to Exploit Underground Space

Singapore has experimented with radical concepts to address our land constraints, especially in the use of underground space. Some of the major experiments include the Underground Ammunition Facility (UAF) of the Singapore Armed Forces, the Deep Tunnel Sewerage System (DTSS), and the Jurong Rock Caverns (JRC).

The success of these experiments convinced the government to exploit underground space systematically, and it has now embarked on developing a comprehensive masterplan for underground space.

At the launch of the Jurong Rock Caverns, PM Lee Hsien Loong made some remarks that I think encapsulate the importance of such an experimental approach:

> We must constantly think out of the box, be bold in tackling our challenges, be tenacious in execution in order to create new space for ourselves whether it is physical space, whether it is space which is metaphorical, thinking space, international space, and development space. It is not just that the sky is the limit, but there are also fewer limits than we think to the depths to which we can go because we are limited only by our own imagination![21]

---

[21] Lee Hsien Loong, "Transcript of Prime Minister Lee Hsien Loong's Speech at the Official Opening of the Jurong Rock Caverns" (speech, Jurong Rock Caverns, Singapore, 2 September 2014), http://www.pmo.gov. sg/newsroom/transcript-prime-minister-lee-hsien-loongs-speech-official-opening-jurong-rock-caverns.

Imagination

This brings me to the importance of imagination.

I recently read a fascinating interview with the famous physicist, Nikola Tesla, the inventor of the alternating current. The interview is dated 30th January 1926. In that interview, Tesla talks about aircraft that will "travel the skies, unmanned, driven and guided by radio." He said that while "motion pictures have been transmitted by wireless over a short distance... later the distance will be illimitable, and by later, I mean only a few years hence."[22] And he thought that "temperate zones will turn frigid or torrid." The world he described nearly a century ago is already upon us — drones, television and climate change.

There are also futures that are not quite with us yet, but they are emerging. In his interview, Tesla spoke of power being "transmitted great distances without wires." And his most fascinating vision was of wireless achieving "closer contact through transmission of intelligence, transport of our bodies and materials and conveyance of energy." In his vision:

> When wireless is perfectly applied, the whole earth will be converted into a huge brain, which in fact it is, all things being particles of a real and rhythmic whole. We shall be able to communicate with one another instantly, irrespective of distance... and the instruments through which we shall be able to do his will be amazingly simple compared with our present telephone. A man will be able to carry one in his vest pocket.[23]

We may not be a single global brain — yet — but our mobile phones certainly do fit into our pockets. In its time, Tesla's description was an amazing feat of imagination. We can aim to make improvements, step-by-step, but for a small country like Singapore, it is better to aim big, in order to stay ahead of the competition. In this regard, imagination is vital.

---

[22] Nikola Tesla, "When Woman is Boss," interview by John B. Kennedy, *Colliers*, 30 January 1926, http://www.tfcbooks.com/tesla/1926-01-30.htm.

[23] Ibid.

Imagination and the Smart Nation

Singapore has a big ambition, to become a Smart Nation.[24] But what is a Smart Nation? At one level, it is about the exploitation of technologies in order to make the lives of people better, by giving them convenient and fast access to information, and to customised services, including those that we cannot even imagine today. The current state of technology already offers all the ingredients of a Smart Nation.

But at another, I would argue, more fundamental level, being a Smart Nation calls for innovation at the systems level — aggregating technologies and combining them with new operating concepts, policies and plans — to solve national problems such as the effects of climate change, traffic congestion, an ageing population, or simply to improve service delivery. But its realisation is the sum of many innovations, big and small. Its ambition should be big, but its implementation is in hundreds and thousands of projects, both large and little.

But at both levels, it is a product of our imagination, and it is only limited by our imagination. Like Nikola Tesla, we can only begin to imagine the endless possible futures.

Imagine a Smart Nation where there is increased efficiency, convenience and connectivity in and between workplaces and homes. Wearable technology such as hologram devices are used on the go to check and respond to work e-mails. Wi-Fi is available island-wide, eliminating restrictions from fixed data and limited call minutes. In the workplace, robots take over routine administrative tasks, coordinating meetings, conducting research and running daily errands. At home, robotic helpers do the household chores and prepare meals. They order groceries when food items are low in stock, which are then delivered by drone to the doorstep. Throughout Singapore, there are healthcare pods deployed island-wide at every housing block. These provide medical diagnosis, dispense medicine and provide simple medical services as well. These make it more convenient for elderly residents who have mobility problems and for those who do not have the time to visit a clinic.

---

[24] The Smart Nation initiative was launched by the government in 2014. Its aim is to improve Singaporeans' lives and build strong communities, through the use of new technology, and by involving citizens, companies, and agencies.

However, government may not be structured to reach this level of imagination and boldness of vision. Some might argue that it is not even its business. Innovation at this level is perhaps better achieved by the private sector, and by individual start-ups with the daring and the ideas.

Empowerment is key. Too much top-down control will kill the spirit of innovation that is central to Smart Nation. Instead, the role of government should be to facilitate such innovation by funding incentives and arrangements, and through flexible, rather than restrictive, regulations.

A good example of this approach is the Monetary Authority of Singapore's establishment of a regulatory sandbox last year to allow FinTech companies to experiment with products and services in an environment where if an experiment fails, "it fails safely and cheaply within controlled boundaries, without widespread adverse consequences."[25]

The government also has a key role in connecting these innovations to their societal environments by encouraging and organising test-bedding and pilots of Smart Nation technologies in real-life settings, and perhaps even by insuring the risk of some of these experiments.

In Singapore, a precinct — One North — is now the site of a major pilot for the use of autonomous vehicles, or driverless cars, testing not just the technologies for the cars, but also for the road furniture. Such experiments and trials are essential because the development of these technologies and their applications need to be test-bedded in real environments. If the pilot is successful, then the programme may be expanded beyond this precinct into the larger national transport system, relieving road congestion and getting people to their destinations faster and more safely and, like Car-Free Sunday SG, helping to realise the vision of a car-lite Singapore.

The Politics of the Smart Nation

But there is a political challenge to such ambition. There are many misconceptions about the technologies associated with a Smart Nation. One big misconception is that absolute privacy and absolute security can be achieved

---

[25] Ravi Menon, "Singapore's FinTech Journey — Where We Are, What Is Next," (speech, Singapore FinTech Festival — FinTech Conference, Singapore, 16 November 2016), http://www.mas.gov.sg/News-and-Publications/Speeches-and-Monetary-Policy-Statements/Speeches/2016/Singapore-FinTech-Journey.aspx.

in a 24/7 online world, constantly surrounded by innumerable sensors and smart objects, all connected to the Internet — the Internet of Things.

As smart objects seek to gather more contextual information on behaviour and actions, the ability of smart devices to analyse people's lives and discover their identities will challenge traditional notions of privacy. Such information can clearly be misused and abused, compromising privacy and security.

There is another related issue — a fear, perhaps irrational in some countries, and rational in others — that the government will exploit these technologies to intrude into the private lives of citizens or to create an Orwellian system of mass state surveillance.

To overcome these misconceptions, a mature discussion is needed, not a polemical one. The government has a central role to play in shaping this discussion. It will have to persuade citizens that the benefits outweigh the risks of exploiting these technologies, and then explain how the risks can be managed. This is clearly in the realm of politics, and the onus must be on the political leadership to convince the people that such fears are misplaced in Singapore. But this can only be achieved if there is trust between the people and the government. As I observed earlier, trust in a fast-changing and complex world — the world of the Anthropocene — is a vital asset to good governance.

Leadership

Before I close, I would like to touch on a critical success factor in the complex world of the Anthropocene, where change is accelerating. Change cannot be avoided. Innovation must be continuous because the world does not stand still. Change and its handmaiden — innovation — must be embraced as an imperative of governance. Furthermore, there is no end point. It is a journey without a fixed destination, because the future is an ever-shifting horizon.

But people dislike change; it is human nature. Change requires *leadership*, because it means leading people out of their comfort zone. Getting them to change is an act of will. The *future-fit* leader has to persuade his people to believe in the need for change, instil confidence in change, and empower his people to change.

Successful leaders of change also make their people brave enough to express their opinions, change their behaviour, take risks, and learn from failure. They tolerate mavericks even if they do not embrace them, because all *future-fit* organisations need mavericks. They are the ones who are prepared to challenge conventional wisdom and come up with the ideas that can change the rules of the game.

Some will argue that leaders should be more tolerant of mavericks. My response to this is "Yes, but only up to a point." A maverick is a maverick only if he is fighting the establishment. If he believes enough in his ideas, he ought to have the courage and conviction of his beliefs to push them, even against resistance. If he gives up the moment he runs into some opposition or official rebuff, then in my book, he is not a maverick. I think this is a sound approach. It is essentially a Darwinian process in which only those who have thought through their ideas, and are prepared to stand up and defend them, deserve the chance of a second hearing. Some mavericks will survive.

Conclusion

In today's world of accelerating change — the Anthropocene — we will need to dare to dream and to experiment with things no one else has done before. We must steel ourselves to embark on journeys of discovery in which the destinations are unknown, and where we must be prepared to cope with unexpected outcomes, to experiment, to manage the risk, to fail, and then to pick ourselves up and keep going.

Thank you.

Question-and-Answer Session

Moderated by
Professor Chan Heng Chee

Chan Heng Chee (CHC): Thank you, Peter, for a very interesting and provocative lecture. I must say that Peter was my boss before. He was Permanent Secretary at the Foreign Ministry when I was Ambassador in Washington. And I always looked forward to Peter's visits to the United States, particularly Washington DC, because his curiosity is great, his interests are immense, and we always met an eclectic collection of people.

At that time, he was already collecting the tools to do the kind of analysis he is doing today. He was talking about futures long before many people in Singapore focused on the subject. So, really, Peter, we are seeing the results of that in your first and second lectures, and all the conversations you have had with some of us who have been lucky to be able to work with you.

Now, it is time for questions. I will take the privilege of being Chair to ask you the first question, Peter, and it is on resilience.

In the concept of resilience, there is government resilience, and there is people resilience. I think there is an inverse relationship between the government's resilience and preparedness, and the people's resilience. The more the government is resilient and prepared, and does everything right — in a way, preventing disasters from happening and picking up things very quickly — the less people have to react.

When the MRT trains first broke down, and Singaporeans were fuming and furious, I was one of those who happened to say, "It is not bad for resilience, you know?" We are learning that we are not perfect. Things are not always going to be all smooth, and how do we react as a people? My question to you is: Is that, in fact, true? That the more resilient a government is, the less resilient people are?

Peter Ho (PH): I think it will be true if the government tries to take on the responsibility of solving all problems on its own, and if, by sheer good luck, they happen to be successful in several of them. Then you will have this mindset that, not only does government know best, but government will solve all our problems. That is, of course, the most dangerous situation in my view, because, as I explained in my first lecture, a lot of our complex, wicked problems — and wicked problems are often crises — cannot depend only on governments providing the solutions. They often require the whole of society — not just the people sector but also the private sector, coming together to tackle those problems. If you do not have that instinct in each sector that you do have a role to play, that you cannot just rely on government to do it, then you have a big problem.

I would say, in my experience, for the things that I had to deal with, including the SARS crisis, there was quite a good balance between the government and the people. The government tried to solve part of it, but it also had to rely on the people, and on the private sector to cope with some of those problems. If it is the government doing everything, then you have got a huge problem in this kind of crises because there are so many things going on at the same time. No government is big enough to deal with these problems alone, and, therefore, you have to leave it to many of the smaller organisations, which are in the private sector, the people, the schools, the individuals, and families, to also play their own roles.

So I accept your proposition, but I think, if the government is smart, it will not allow that to happen. Because when you look at the big challenges, that is where the government has begun to learn that it must engage the civil society and private sector. If it tries to do everything on its own, just to score political points, then it has got a problem.

CHC: Thank you, Peter. Questions from the floor?

Participant: I would like to ask about Smart Nation and income inequality. As of now, I feel that Artificial Intelligence (AI) is still not an extremely disruptive thing to our society. But even after taxes and transfers, our GINI coefficient is more than 0.4. In the future, with increasing AI and the Smart Nation initiative, would they worsen our income inequality? And do you think that our government is doing enough to address this problem?

PH: I am not sure how I would connect income inequality necessarily with AI. We are still looking at Artificial Intelligence at the very early stages. It has, undoubtedly, in the last couple of years, made huge leaps forward. In fact, just think about some of the things that have been happening. I think it was 1997 when Deep Blue, the IBM computer, beat Garry Kasparov, the world chess champion at that time. But that was just sheer computing power — number-crunching. Then, 20 years later, AlphaGo beat the South Korean World *Go* champion. This was remarkable, because *Go* is supposed to be a much more complex game than chess, and it was not number-crunching; it was Artificial Intelligence. That was the big difference. And then earlier this year, they announced this AI system that went on to beat world poker champions, which is an even more challenging task.

I have been watching this AI issue, and it has only been in the last few years that AI is really beginning to take off. But the kind of capabilities it is going to provide — where it is going to be used — nobody really knows at this stage. Clearly, it has got huge applications in areas like health provision; it has got possibly a very important application in professional areas like law, and also in things like manufacturing and urban planning. AI obviously shows promise in all these areas, but how it is going to evolve, nobody knows. And what people worry about is not so much, I would say, the risk of creating more income inequality. In fact, I could make an argument that it would actually help reduce some of this inequality, by making these services a lot more accessible to ordinary folk.

But the big concern is, what happens when you start getting systems that are so smart that they start designing themselves, and they design themselves to be better? And the human being does not have a clue as to how the system is thinking — whether it is thinking in a human way, or if it is thinking in some other way. A friend of mine who runs an AI-related research institute had some visitors at the institute, and somebody asked him to show an example of how this new form of intelligence works. So they showed it a picture of two polar bear cubs and asked the AI system, "What are these?" I guess after a bit of thinking about it, the system came back with this answer: "Two puppies, playing in snow."

Now, the researchers there had no clue how the system arrived at the answer. All they knew is that it had never been shown a picture of polar bears. But somehow, it was able to discern that these polar bear cubs were the young of some animal, so they interpreted them to be puppies. The system furthermore saw white, so it assumed that these were puppies playing in snow. Things are going on in Artificial Intelligence that even the researchers themselves do not know, because clearly, AI, which is different from number-crunching, and even different from machine-learning, is going in a way that people find very difficult to understand, because you cannot apply the human framework to understand what is going on.

This is a long way of saying, first, I think Artificial Intelligence is at its very early stages, and it is going to be a very interesting area, so we had better pay a lot of attention to it. It is going to be something we need to get into, but we are going to have to understand the risks. I do not think we should be overly concerned with issues relating to income inequality at this stage. If you ask me, the issues are much more related to ethical issues and how you govern some of these experiments and developments in Artificial Intelligence.

Participant: In a VUCA world, we have seen increasing political fluctuations and unpredictability, even in stable and seemingly resilient countries, for example in the United States, moving rapidly from an Obama administration to a Trump administration, or the United Kingdom, going for a hard Brexit. What are the political risks for the Singapore government, which it should prepare for, and how can officials mitigate these risks?

PH: The point is that you cannot predict the future. And so there will be a whole spectrum of issues you should be worried about. But in the end, what are the issues you have got to worry about? It is a matter of judgment. What will Singapore need to worry about? You can start thinking about not just the political challenges but also the economic challenges. Let us just take the political side. What does it mean when society's expectations of government change? And they are changing, as I mentioned in my lecture, because we have jumped very rapidly from a third-world country where all the people wanted was mostly, "You give me a job, you give me a roof above my head, I get enough food to eat, that is good enough." Very simple.

Now what does it mean when you are at the top of Maslow's hierarchy? What does it mean when we talk about transcendence? Transcendence means helping somebody else achieve his full potential. How does government help in this sort of thing? It is a reality we have to deal with.

Then there are of course, other issues and uncertainties. Technology and climate change are two big uncertainties. Our demographics are also a big uncertainty because, not only are we grappling with this problem of a low Total Fertility Rate (TFR), but also the problem of an ageing population. Each has its own challenges that have to be dealt with. How do you integrate this into a coherent policy that may not entirely satisfy everybody, but reasonably satisfy the core and most critical issues?

These are just some of the challenges that government are going to face. I would say the fundamental point is, there are no easy answers. You cannot just look in a crystal ball, and say, "This is going to be the future." You will often get it wrong. So if you cannot be sure what is going to happen, you have to think about many alternatives, and out of these, decide on the ones you are going to focus on. It is always a matter of judgment — you never get anything 100 per cent right.

CHC: Peter, apropos the last question. One of my colleagues at the Lee Kuan Yew Centre for Innovative Cities, in SUTD, was just visited by three students from another university, who came to have a chat with her. They were talking about diversity and my colleague asked the students what they read. The three students said they did not read anything about Singapore. She asked, "Why?" They said it is because Singapore is so stable, and the government will take care of things anyway.

But they read up a lot about the United States because of President Trump, and they did not know what was going to happen. Everything seemed so volatile, and they were worried about their jobs.

PH: I think every government is not just worried about what is going on within their country. A country like Singapore, in particular, because of our size and geostrategic situation, actually has to worry a lot about the external environment, which, in today's context, is a very volatile environment. All the familiar markers are disappearing, and it is becoming more and more challenging. Where we will end up, I do not know.

The big question is whether we are just passing through a phase, whether this is a blip, or whether this is a fundamental re-ordering of the world. We do not really know, and we may not know for some years to come. So these are all questions the government will have to think about.

Participant: Singapore's first 50 modern years was built largely on discipline; on very severe discipline, in some cases. That is really what made it successful. Today, achieving the creative imagination and the consensus for it requires a different mindset. Are we devoting enough time and effort to teaching the young creative disobedience?

PH: Well, in a way, I am going to address this in my next two lectures, so I do not want to reveal too much. But you do raise an important point. There is this stereotyped image of the Singaporean, who is very obedient, follows rules, will do what he is told, and is not very imaginative. Some people say it is true. I actually have quite a different take on this. I think the younger generation, who are very different from my generation, and certainly very different from what we call the pioneer generation, are far more able to express themselves. And they express themselves not only because they have platforms like the social media, which is very critical, but because they are much better educated today. They know what the issues are. Many of them do their homework. Some of them do not, and then that is where you get some trouble separating the wheat from the chaff. But there are those who do their homework properly, and then you are in a situation where the government not only has to listen to them, because they have come up with persuasive arguments, but the government also finds value in some of their insights.

Society itself is changing very fast. The question is: Can the government keep up with the pace of change? See, the point I am trying to make here is the pace of change. If things are moving, as I said, at a velocity, then it is not so difficult. You know, you sit down, analyse anything and everything, and that kind of works out reasonably well. But things are changing so fast. What looks like a sound approach today may no longer work tomorrow because people's expectations have changed again, and you are constantly trying to keep up.

But coming back to the young generation. I do not know whether any of you have visited the JTC Launchpad, which is just on the other side of the road from here. It is remarkable. You look at the young Singaporeans who are prepared to take some of their ideas, and have the conviction to try them out, even if they are not sure of any kind of success. I have met some people I know with stable jobs in government, who say, "I believe in what I am doing, I am prepared to try it out." And some of them will succeed, some of them will fail.

But the fact that the JTC Launchpad is successful tells you that there are quite a lot of Singaporeans who are willing to show that kind of guts and gumption, which you need, to be innovative. So I am a bit more optimistic.

Participant: I want to tie the question back to the question on inequality. One of the things you mentioned is driverless cars. As we all know, it is not so much driverless cars among commuters. It is actually driverless cars in public transport. Imagine that in maybe 10, 20 years, cars will be driverless. We have taxi drivers, bus drivers, and of course we have truck drivers. All these people will be displaced. There is no need for all of them. So their jobs are gone! Clearly there will be some inequalities.

The other example I can give is on retail. We know that for retail in Singapore, you can see a lot of the malls empty nowadays because many of the people have gone online. So again, jobs in retail services are probably disappearing. There will be large job losses and displacement. One possible solution that people are thinking of right now — where there are no jobs, is this concept of the UBI, this Universal Basic Income. Everybody gets money from the government, and it is being tried in Finland, Holland, and of course was rejected in Switzerland just recently. Would Singapore be thinking of UBI?

PH: Well, I do not know whether they are thinking about it, but I am sure the thought has crossed their mind. Now look, the issue is not so much whether all these technologies are going to create displacement. They are. There is no doubt.

I was in London recently, and I was sitting in one of those famous London black cabs. He was telling me, complaining bitterly about disruptions caused by Uber. He said, "You know, in London, there are something like 26,000 black taxi cabs. We have 'The Knowledge'.[26] What is The Knowl-

---

[26] "The Knowledge of London" is a course that licensed London taxi drivers have to pass. It was introduced in 1865.

edge? The Knowledge is the ability to get from point A to point B without having to refer to any kind of map or any kind of device. We spend five years acquiring it."

Here comes an Uber driver who has his little iPhone or some other navigation device. He does not need The Knowledge. He just asks where you want to go, keys in the destination, and the iPhone or the smartphone will tell him how to get there. And my black cab driver told me something quite interesting. He said, three years ago, there were hardly any of these cars. Now there are 90,000 Uber cars.

I do not know how accurate he is, but these are 90,000 Uber cars on the road compared to 26,000 black cabs. Of course this is disruptive. What are you going to do? What does the government do? They try to make sure there is a level playing field, but they cannot say, "Stop the march of technology, stop the advance of this kind of service", for which there is great demand. Otherwise there will not be 90,000 Uber cars on the road!

So when you ask that question about income inequality, I think it is a loaded question. Of course people will be disrupted, but that does not mean it is necessarily negative. If you say, you want to freeze everything — no progress, no technology, because it is just too disruptive, then that is it! There will be consequences that come with that kind of approach.

But if you say, well, there is going to be some disruption but let us think about how we can manage it. Because the underlying issue is, the pace of change is accelerating. And if you do not understand the implications of this, then of course you will be worried about all these things, without thinking about what we do when change accelerates. You cannot predict which types of jobs will be affected. You get some sense of where the jobs are going to be disrupted, or where they are going to be affected. But you cannot be sure what form this disruption will take, and of course with new technologies, there will be new opportunities! It is not as if there are no new opportunities that are created when something gets disrupted. That is why one of the important points is that you have to reskill all the time.

I remember reading a report about the United States. They said in today's economy, which is changing very fast, a typical worker will, in his lifetime, change his job four to five times. Not because of choice, but because of sunset and sunrise industries, created by new technologies and demand.

If that is the reality, then you have to keep on retraining the people. That is why we should not underplay the significance of the SkillsFuture initiative. Because you do not know what is going to happen, but you recognise that you have to create a capacity to the system, to help people retrain. And training when you are 18 is very different from training when you are 30, or 40, or 50 years old. There are different priorities. When you are 30 years old, you are starting a family; you have got mortgages to worry about, and so on. That is a different type of challenge, but people would still need help.

Participant: What is the relationship between what you talked about, the challenges you talked about, and the future? And by defining what those challenges are, in some ways, the government is also the one setting out the imagination — the social imagination of Singapore — in terms of those challenges. How does that allow for dissensus over what future we can choose?

PH: Is that a new word, "dissensus"?

Participant: The opposite of what consensus is.

CHC: Dissensus as opposed to consensus. It is about the official definition of challenges and where is the space for dissensus, right?

Participant: Yes. And if I may have one more question, what would you not take from the concepts of the Anthropocene or resilience? While they claim to be universal concepts, you need to recognise their provenance, which, going by the examples you have given, mostly come from the global North and largely come from countries like the United States or Britain.

PH: Let me first deal with your question on dissensus versus consensus. I do not know whether it is a new word — some people are saying it is.

I think things have changed in Singapore. It is fair to say that, in the early years, it was very much a top-down kind of system where "government knows best" and the government decided that "these are the big issues" and "these are the challenges". In fact, there had been hardly any disagreement about what the big issues were in those days anyway. Even if we had a kind of big townhall meeting, and everybody sat down, they would be worried about the same issues. Maybe slightly nuanced, but they would be worried about housing, jobs, and things like that.

But today, it is a much more diverse society. Opinions about the way forward, and what the challenges are, I would say, are much more fragmented. And sometimes you can be confused because of the Internet. Whoever uses the social media effectively tends to get a much louder voice, and then you think that this is how everybody looks at the issue when, in fact, it sometimes is not the case.

So how does the government deal with that? Not easy! They watch the social media, but they also have to have their townhall meetings, they have to get a sense of people's worries. I do not mean to go back to Our Singapore Conversation, but it was a very important step forward, because that was where you heard what the people were really worried about. And what emerged out of Our Singapore Conversation, which took place from 2012 to 2013? What emerged were very clear indications of what the people were worried about. It was not the government saying this is what the people are worried about — it was people saying what they were worried about. What were they worried about? If I remember, it was housing, health, transport, and jobs. I cannot remember — there were four big issues.[27] This was the people saying what they were worried about. It was not the government saying, "Oh, I want you to worry about this, I want you to worry about that."

So we should not think that the government is deaf to the people. Maybe in other countries, but I think after 2011, the Singapore government said, maybe we had better listen to the people. It is a process. And do not forget, in the economic arena, we have had a far longer track record than in the social arena. With all these economic review committees, the government actually listens to what the private sector says, and what the academics say, about the economy. Everything is on the table! There are no sacred cows. You can say whatever you want to say. The track record is really quite an interesting story, which is often not told. Very few governments, in my view and experience, actually have done things like that, where they open up the whole economic policy for open and honest debate.

Now, you talked about tools of the Anthropocene — what was it…?

CHC: … do you accept every concept.

---

[27] The three main priorities concerning Singaporeans in the Our Singapore Conversation survey were housing, healthcare and jobs. Transport was a key priority for participants earning less than S$3,000.

PH: Do I accept every concept?

CHC: He clearly does — he put it in his lecture!

PH: I am not entirely sure, can you explain what the issue is?

Participant: The question is, from what you have read about the Anthropocene and resilience, is there anything from those books or materials that you would not accept?

PH: I only bring in the Anthropocene as a device to help us understand why the era we are in is an era of very rapid change. And rapid change brings special challenges to governance. That is the fundamental issue. It is not whether I am going to debate the best scientific minds about whether the Anthropocene exists, whether it started with the Industrial Age, or whether it started with the Great Acceleration in the 1950s. That is not the point.

The real point is, we are in a very unusual period of time, and if the pace of change continues this way, it is going to have huge implications for the ability to govern. How do you govern when things are changing every few years? Technologies are disrupting themselves, and these disruptions are happening every few years! It is a great challenge for governments. That is the issue — it is not about whether I am going to debate the existence of Anthropocene or not. But anyway, I actually do believe the Anthropocene exists.

Participant: Singaporeans, I think, have a good streak of creative disobedience. If you look on SGAG, you can see a lot of examples where Singaporeans are really creative in very different ways. My question is whether it is possible for the Singapore government to maintain an organisation like Skunk Works, which is prepared to implement projects, and fail fast and safe fail, so that we can try out as many techniques as possible. It will also be an organisation that fulfils the role of testing crises or testing disruptive technologies across our agencies, which will help to provide some sort of integration across the different agencies.

PH: I think I understand this question because at least I am familiar with Skunk Works. Skunk Works, for the rest of the audience, was a very experimental outfit within Lockheed. It was given a very special mandate to rapidly prototype all kinds of new weapon systems to sell to the American military. Some of the star outcomes were things like stealth fighters and I cannot remember the name, their high-altitude reconnaissance aircraft.[28]

So that was very successful, but I must tell you that, when you look at Skunk Works, remember that there is another lesson: other companies tried to replicate Skunk Works, including Boeing, but none of them succeeded the way Lockheed Skunk Works succeeded. It is a combination of both very strong visionary leadership — not just the visionary leadership of Lockheed, but the visionary leadership of Skunk Works itself — and also the kind of resources and strong support that it was given. Because in this kind of environment, failure is going to be part and parcel of trying things out. So we talk very blithely about trying these kinds of experiments, but we have to accept that there is going to be failure.

Now, governments are actually in a very peculiar position. If there is failure — and even if we accept the logic of experimentation — politically, sometimes, the electorate will be very unforgiving when there is a failure, in spite of the fact that the government says, "Look, I told you right at the start, this is an experiment, it may or may not succeed!" What is the government to do? Do not try anything out? But you know, each time they fail, they are conditioned to be a bit more careful the next time round. So boldness is very important, and it is boldness that actually helped Lockheed Skunk Works to make their achievements, but it does not happen everywhere.

I gave you the examples of DARPA, and the Future Systems Directorate, which MINDEF established, and arguably helped create the third generation SAF. When I was still in service, I wondered whether we could do something like that for government as a whole. And my conclusion was we could not do it. It is just too complex to manage. You have to really rely on individual agencies to decide what are the things worth doing, and they, if necessary, set up their own Skunk Works, or the equivalent of the Future Systems Directorate.

But this is always a balance — you cannot mandate this kind of thing. It has just got to be somebody with the idea, having the guts and gumption to drive it, and then it happens. But it does not happen all the time. Just

---

[28] These were the U2 and the SR71 Blackbird.

because you see one successful example does not mean it is going to be successful every time it is replicated. So you have to be very practical about this sort of thing.

CHC: Well, Peter, you have really stimulated the audience. Now I am supposed to draw this to a close and say a few words, which is really very difficult because it has been such a wide-ranging lecture.

But what I have heard is clearly that there is discomfort with the rapid advancement of technology, and how we should react to this. This is not a wrong sense to get, because everywhere, people are talking about this. I have heard Silicon Valley people who invest in start-ups — technologists, who now talk about social responsibility for the use of technology. So that question is now beginning to occur to people who deal with technology, and Bill Gates said, maybe we should tax robots. I remember seeing Peter put out as a slide: Hawking, Elon Musk, and Gates, talking about their concerns with the AI. That fear, that concern, is not a misplaced one. That is one question that will be emerging more and more. And what do you do with, how do you deal with, technology. It will come, and you will have to embrace it. But how do you embrace it smartly, and work with it, and try to minimise the disruption for our society?

The second point I want to make here, Peter, is that you have laid out all these concepts for the VUCA world. Things we have to react to: black swans, white elephants, you know, resilience — black elephants, sorry! Actually, people talk of the orange elephant in the United States because he is so suntanned. But the point is, all these are concepts, and all our bureaucrats are exposed to this now.

The question I have that I do not require you to answer now, Peter, is this: Whilst we understand the concepts, how do we weave it into our work? And how do you actually prepare for it? Look at David Cameron! Look at what he did. The Brexit referendum — how did he ever face this black swan or black elephant or whatever it is? He made the gravest mistake of his career, a historic mistake. So as bureaucrats, even if you know these concepts, how do you implement policy, and between knowing, and action and behaviour, how do you change behaviour?

I think we still do not understand that, but thank you very much, for your exposition of all these wonderful ideas.

Lecture III

THE PARADOX OF SINGAPORE AND THE DIALECTIC OF GOVERNANCE

Introduction

F ew countries today would be classified as sovereign and independent city states. And rightly so, because their continuing existence is a special challenge.

Cities like Hong Kong are sometimes referred to as city states because of their high degree of autonomy, but they are neither sovereign nor independent. The consensus is that only Singapore, together with Monaco and Vatican City, are true independent city states. Even then, only Singapore has all the attributes of a sovereign state, in particular, because it is fully responsible for its own defence. In contrast, Monaco depends on France for its defence, and Vatican City, on Italy.

Looking back in history, there are the famous city states of antiquity, like Athens, Sparta and Carthage. In medieval times, the standout is Venice. For centuries, the city of Venice was a flourishing centre of trade between Europe and Asia, especially in silk, grain and spices. By the 13th century, Venice had become Europe's second largest city, after Paris, and its most prosperous.

But as former Foreign Minister George Yeo observed:

... Venice never felt invulnerable. She never took her success for granted. It was this sense of insecurity which spurred her on, which kept her guards up, her citizens united and her institutions vital.[1]

Perhaps the central and most obvious *paradox of Singapore* is that its national boundaries coincide perfectly with its city limits. And what is more, the fantasy and glamour of Singapore's global city status often stand in sharp contrast to the insecurities that define its statehood.

Sovereign city states are anomalies, surviving despite their very small size, without natural resource, and surrounded by much larger neighbours. Their existence is a constant struggle with challenges that larger nations with hinterlands and resources do not worry about. They are a paradox, the exceptions that prove the rule that size matters.

An Accidental Country, an Improbable Nation

Singapore's sudden elevation to the status of sovereign city state was an accident of history — an unintended consequence of the politics of the time. Singapore was never conceived of as an independent nation. Our *raison d'être* had been as a service centre for regional trade, and a trading outpost of the British Empire. In 1957, Mr Lee Kuan Yew observed that "island-nations are political jokes."[2] In 1962, the Singapore government described the merger of Singapore into the Federation of Malaysia as an "*inevitable* historical development".[3]

Indeed, if things had gone the way Mr Lee and his colleagues had intended, Singapore would still be a part of Malaysia. In an oral history

---

[1] George Yeo Yong-Boon, Asad Latif, and Huiling Li, *George Yeo on Bonsai, Banyan and the Tao* (Singapore: World Scientific, 2015), 16.

[2] Singapore Legislative Assembly, *Debates III*, no. 20 (5 March 1957), col. 1,471.

[3] Lee Kuan Yew, "Summary of the Case of the Singapore Government by the Prime Minister, Mr. Lee Kuan Yew, Disposing of Points Made by the Representatives of the 19 Singapore Assemblymen who Appeared Before the Committee Earlier in the Morning of the Same Day," (speech, Singapore, 26 July 1962), National Archives of Singapore, http://www.nas.gov.sg/archivesonline/data/pdfdoc/lky19620726c.pdf.

interview in 1982, Mr S Rajaratnam spoke about the Singaporean leaders' conflicted feelings on Separation. He said:

> *Emotionally we were still rejecting it. But intellectually, as I said, we had no choice ... we ourselves believed that an independent Singapore is not viable. That was not a device just to have merger. But I think it was a genuine basic belief. So now we had to prove that what we believed in, is not necessarily so.*[4]

From Third World to First

And Singapore soon could make concrete claims to success. Gross Domestic Product (GDP) jumped from US$974 million in 1965, to US$36.2 billion in 1990. After 50 years, GDP stood at US$292.7 billion. Life expectancy has increased by about 10 years every generation, from 64.5 years in 1965, to 75.3 years in 1990, and now, 82.7 years. That Singapore moved from Third World to First within two generations — less than 50 years — is without precedent and nothing short of a modern miracle.

Envy and Admiration: The Little Red Dot

Singapore's success has evoked much admiration. One of the early admirers was the late Deng Xiaoping, who visited Singapore as Senior Vice-Premier in 1978. He was greatly interested in Singapore's social and economic development experience. Deng saw how Singapore, without natural resources, had been able to provide a good life for its people through good governance, and to create jobs through pragmatic policies aimed at bringing in foreign investment. This inspired Deng to embrace the market economy.

But Singapore has had its share of detractors. In an interview with the *Asian Wall Street Journal* in August 1998, then Indonesian President B J Habibie dismissed Singapore as just "a little red dot", with only three million people then, compared to Indonesia's "sea of green",[5] with its population of over 200 million.

---

[4]S Rajaratnam, "Rajaratnam, S, 26 July 1982," (interview, 26 July 1982), National Archives of Singapore, http://www.nas.gov.sg/archivesonline/viewer?uuid=c8215047-1160-11e3-83d5-0050568939ad-OHC000149_015.
[5]Richard Borsuk and Reginald Chua, "Singapore Strains Relations with Indonesia's President," *The Asian Wall Street Journal*, 4 August 1998.

Instead of being intimidated, Singapore has embraced this disparaging put-down as a badge of honour. A few months after Mr Habibie's remarks, then Deputy Prime Minister Lee Hsien Loong was quoted in *The Jakarta Post* as saying:

> *A little red dot is not an issue, (it's a) geographical fact we are small, without resources (while) the population is small, but we have to make a living.*[6]

And Singaporeans do so, as *The Economist* described it in a 2015 report, "with a characteristic mix of pride and paranoia."[7] Indeed, the criticism of paranoia has been levelled at Singapore many times. In particular, many observers refer to our attitude towards defence and foreign policy as part of a "siege mentality", or *kiasu-ism* if you will. But arguably, if Singapore was not *kiasu*,[8] we would likely not have survived to celebrate 50 years of independence in 2015.

Overcoming Our Fundamental Vulnerabilities

At independence, there were huge challenges to overcome: our small size, a heterogeneous and migrant population without any sense of nationhood, our lack of natural resources, and a geopolitical vulnerability stemming from the double minority situation, as a Chinese-majority state in a predominantly Malay world.

But struggle is a Darwinian process, in which only the strong — and strong-minded — survive. It was our water scarcity that led us to develop water treatment technologies that we now export to other parts of the world, including the Middle East, Latin America, and Africa. Our shortage of land, poor urban conditions, and severe lack of safe and quality housing led us to develop urban planning solutions, and both high-rise as well as under-ground space. Our lack of strategic depth impelled us to acquire or develop

---

[6] Kornelius Purba, "RI Asked to Continue Lead ASEAN Role," *The Jakarta Post*, 2 November 1998.
[7] *The Economist*, "A Little Red Dot in a Sea of Green," http://www.economist.com/news/special-report/21657610-sense-vulnerability-has-made-singapore-what-it-today-can-it-now-relax-bit
[8] *Kiasu* is a Hokkien term for being afraid of losing out and being overly competitive.

sophisticated bespoke defence systems, and innovative training models and arrangements with friendly countries to overcome this challenge.

But this does not mean that our fundamental problems have been solved. Our small size and low-lying position make us extremely vulnerable to climate change. Our high global rankings, such as being the world's busiest port by shipping tonnage, are constantly tested by geopolitical and geo-economic developments. Even though we have developed new technologies in our water security, as former PUB Chairman Tan Gee Paw once noted, our great challenges in water management are climate change and complacency among our populace.[9]

The Singapore Paradox

Singapore's parlous geo-strategic position has been the driving force for the country to find ways to overcome these challenges. As a result, today, we have the heft to make our way in the world and to wield some influence. But obviously, we cannot assume that we have overcome our vulnerabilities. In that sense, Singapore, more so than most, is a perpetual work-in-progress. With SG50 came a slew of articles examining Singapore's "exceptionalism". *The Economist* summed up our challenges ahead:

> *Its leaders hold themselves to high standards. But it is debatable whether the system Mr Lee built can survive in its present form.*[10]

All the unfavourable conditions that attended Singapore's unexpected elevation to sovereign city state still exist today. But our success in overcoming them may well have masked the deep challenges that remain, and remain mostly undiminished. This is the *paradox of Singapore*.

The Little Red Dot or the Apple of Nations?

In 2010, my friend, the futurist Peter Schwartz, described Singapore as the "Apple of Nations".[11] He was not using "apple" in its idiomatic form, but

---

[9] Tan Gee Paw, *Singapore Chronicles: Water* (Singapore: Straits Times Press, 2016), 89.
[10] Simon Long, "The Singapore Exception," *The Economist*, 18 July 2015, http://www.economist.com/news/special-report/21657606-continue-flourish-its-second-half-century-south-east-asias-miracle-city-state.
[11] Peter Schwartz, "Singapore: The Apple of Nations," *Ethos*: Issue 7, January 2010, https://www.cscollege.gov.sg/Knowledge/Ethos/Issue%207%20Jan%202010/Pages/Singapore-The-Apple-of-Nations.aspx.

favourably comparing Singapore as a nation to Apple the company, which was then, as now, an inspiring paragon of innovation. Apple is famous for its innovative and revolutionary products. Many think that this year Apple will become the first trillion-dollar company in terms of market capitalisation.

It was high praise from Schwartz. But of course, it begs the question of whether we can truly be the Apple of Nations, or whether we are in reality just a Little Red Dot. Schwartz, who is no rosy-eyed admirer of Singapore, also warned:

> *The difference between Apple and Singapore is that the people of Singapore don't know how good they have it. They don't know just what a remarkable entity has been created here. They don't share yet that sense of passion that the people at Apple do.*[12]

This concern was echoed in Prime Minister Lee Hsien Loong's 2016 National Day Rally speech, when he said:

> *What I would like to have is that we be blessed with a "divine discontent" — always not quite satisfied with what we have, always driven to do better. At the same time, we have the wisdom to count our blessings so that we know how precious Singapore is and we know how to enjoy it and to protect it.*[13]

Dialectic of Governance

I endeavoured to establish in my first two lectures that our operating environment is a fast-changing and complex one. It is to lead to the fundamental question of how Singapore can survive and succeed as a sovereign and independent city state.

There are clearly no easy answers. It is very easy to criticise from the side, but it is not at all easy to find the right answers. Each big decision and every major policy is not an exercise in finding the absolute right answer. It is always an exercise in making the right judgment — a balanced one that

[12] Lee Hsien Loong, "National Day Rally 2016 Speech," (speech, ITE College Central, Singapore, 21 August 2016), Prime Minister's Office, http://www.pmo.gov.sg/national-day-rally-2016-speech-english-part-2.
[13] Peter Schwartz, "Singapore: The Apple of Nations."

serves the larger interests of the majority and of the country. And even that judgement must change, because the operating environment is changing, not at the pace of velocity, but at the rate of an acceleration.

I shall use the *dialectical* method to try to extract some insights, if not answers, to this question. A dialectic is a discourse between two or more people holding different points of view about a subject. Both sides, however, share the same goal of establishing truth through well-reasoned arguments. It is through such discourse that perhaps some answers will emerge about what it takes for Singapore to survive and succeed over the long term.

Big Government *Versus* Small Government

Thrust into an unwelcome and unwanted independence, the Singapore government was in a hurry to turn the precarious situation around, and to transform Singapore into a "modern metropolis", in the matchless pledge of Mr Lee Kuan Yew in 1965.

So, it is not surprising that in the beginning, governance in Singapore was characterised by *big government*, if you will, through strong regulation, seeking compliance with policy rules, and maintaining as efficient a system as possible, in order to get things moving and to get them done.

Through this approach, the government embarked on a number of major initiatives that helped to lay the foundations for Singapore's prosperity and stability. These included a massive public housing programme; heavy investments in infrastructure — in public transport, our port and airport; and an activist, government-led approach to attract foreign investments and build up the capabilities to support higher value-added activities.

In these and many other policy domains, the visible hand of government was as critical as the invisible hand of markets. The government's interventions enabled new markets and industries to develop. They also helped to ensure that economic growth throughout the 1970s and 1980s benefited all segments of the population.

Some see this as the Singapore government exercising substantial influence not just over traditional areas of policy, like defence, macroeconomics and infrastructure, but also in areas like tree-planting and compulsory savings, which are seen as more municipal or personal in other countries.

The ban on the sale of chewing gum has been cited by many as an example of a pervasive and intrusive government role.

Mr Lee Kuan Yew made no bones about his belief that government should intervene in a spectrum of issues. He famously said:

> *I am often accused of interfering in the private lives of citizens. Yes, if I did not, had I not done that, we wouldn't be here today. And I say without the slightest remorse, that we wouldn't be here, we would not have made economic progress, if we had not intervened on very personal matters — who your neighbour is, how you live, the noise you make, how you spit, or what language you use. We decide what is right. Never mind what the people think.*[14]

Government Spending

But on many significant measures, Singapore's government is not at all big. The Washington think tank, the Heritage Foundation, together with the *Wall Street Journal*, compiles an annual "Index of Economic Freedom", measuring several dimensions of a country's economic freedom.

One of these dimensions is the size of government spending, which in Singapore has been very low for a country of our level of development. According to the most recent Index of Economic Freedom, total government expenditure in Singapore constituted 18.2 per cent of GDP.[15] This is among the lowest in the world. In comparison, Hong Kong's total government expenditure amounted to 18.3 per cent of GDP, and it does not have to spend on defence. In New Zealand, which was ranked third behind Hong Kong and Singapore for economic freedom, government expenditure totalled 42.2 per cent of GDP.

Evolution of Government in Singapore

The system of government in Singapore was inherited from the British — actually, from the British East India Company, the pre-eminent global multinational corporation of the day that Sir Stamford Raffles worked for.

---

[14] Lee Kuan Yew, "National Day Rally 1986 Speech," (speech, Kallang Theatre, Singapore, 17 August 1986), National Archives of Singapore, http://www.nas.gov.sg/archivesonline/audiovisual_records/record-details/48aabfb1-1164-11e3-83d5-0050568939ad.

[15] The Heritage Foundation, "2017 Index of Economic Freedom," (n.d.) http://www.heritage.org/index/country/singapore.

So, it is not as if we started from scratch. Because of these antecedents, it is natural that Singapore looks to developments in administrations that are based on the Westminster system of government. It is not surprising that the practice of governance in Singapore has broadly tracked the trajectories of other governments in countries like Australia, Canada, New Zealand, and especially in the United Kingdom, the birthplace of the Westminster system of government. Nevertheless, it has always been to adapt, and not to adopt blindly.

Influence of Thatcherism

Margaret Thatcher became Prime Minister of Great Britain in 1979. She was a strong believer in small government — as opposed to big government — and in the ability of the private sector to provide goods and services more efficiently. She believed in reducing the role of the state in the economy. In her worldview, the private sector was often better placed to deliver public services, and market forces should be given a free hand, and entrepreneurial energies unshackled. In taking such a *laissez-faire* approach towards regulating the private sector, it is argued that small government lowers costs and promotes efficiency by allowing the market to determine prices and economic outcomes.

The underlying philosophy of Thatcherism had a huge impact, and influenced governments around the world, including Singapore's. So, in the 1990s, the Singapore government began changing its approach, focused on creating a leaner public administration while delivering better services.

To this end, the government sought to harness the creativity and dynamism of the private sector to deliver public services, and to achieve efficiency gains from the forces of competition. It explored ways in which government could divest its interests and allow for entrepreneurial energies to flourish. The privatisation of our state-owned utilities began with Singapore Telecoms in 1993. This was followed by the liberalisation of the telecommunications sector. In the electricity sector, our own privatisation and liberalisation experience was also very much influenced by the experience of the British government, particularly in its decision to vertically separate the industry.

Networked Government

But things do not stand still. This is, after all, the Anthropocene and the era of the Great Acceleration. The 1990s also saw another evolution in the thinking about government. The focus shifted towards integrated or joined-up government — one that coordinates efforts across departments, harnesses new information technologies, and partners the private sector to deliver better services.

David Osborne and Ted Gaebler, in their groundbreaking book *Reinventing Government*, wrote:

> *The governments we saw that steered more and rowed less — like St. Paul — were clearly stronger governments. After all, those who steer the boat have far more power over its destination than those who row it.*[16]

The aim was no longer to shrink governments, but to emulate best practices in the corporate world to stay relevant. These would include adopting new technologies, embracing principles of customer-centric design, and giving greater attention to customer experience. The aim instead was to make governments more effective, more efficient, and more focused on delivering better services to their customers in the private and people sectors.

In this context, many services that government provides require agencies to work together. This is often described as "networked government", which is the synthesis of four trends:

- *Joined-up government* that is aimed at providing integrated service through getting multiple government agencies to join together. The Economic Development Board's much admired — and copied — concept of the "one-stop shop" is an example of joined-up government. Potential investors only have to deal with a single point of contact, rather than a plethora of approving agencies. Of course, creating a *one-stop shop* requires a lot of coordination in the backroom among various agencies and ministries.

---

[16] David Osborne and Ted Gaebler, *Reinventing Government: How the Entrepreneurial Spirit is Transforming the Public Sector* (Reading, Mass: Addison-Wesley, 1992), 32.

It requires them to work together in a networked, coordinated fashion. The alternative is a bloated bureaucracy, slow service and frustrated customers.

- *The digital revolution* in which advances in infocomm technologies are harnessed to enable government agencies to share information, exchange data and collaborate in real time with other government agencies and with external partners to deliver faster and more accurate services to the public.
- *Outsourcing* by using private firms and non-profit organisations — as opposed to just using government employees — to deliver better services and achieve policy goals.
- *Increasing consumer sophistication* leading to increased citizen demand for more control over their lives and more choice in their public services, to match the customised service provision that already exists in the private sector.

Whole-of-Government

The *Whole-of-Government* approach, which I introduced in my first lecture, is a natural evolution from networked government. With a mindset of more integrated collaboration already established among government agencies through networked government, Whole-of-Government has emerged in Singapore at least as an important response to managing complexity and dealing with wicked problems.

In this approach, instead of breaking down a wicked problem into smaller parts, and then leaving it to each agency to make its own, decentralised and bounded decisions, Whole-of-Government promotes not just backroom coordination to provide public services in a more efficient manner. But it also emphasises sharing of information among ministries, statutory boards and other agencies, at the strategic level, in order to take in different ideas and insights. This is so that wicked problems can be viewed in their manifold dimensions, and so that the appropriate policy prescriptions and plans can be developed.

Government *Versus* Governance

Today, citizens and businesses alike have far higher expectations of government than before. Access to information has increased dramatically in scope and speed as a result of the Internet revolution. Social networking platforms like Facebook, YouTube and Twitter have empowered citizens to express their views. Virtual communities are beginning to shape the debate and context of public policy issues.

The view that "government knows best" that perhaps characterised the situation in the beginning is increasingly challenged in today's world, in which citizens and businesses can easily gain access to much of the information that governments used to monopolise and control in the past.

The Future of Government in Singapore

Today, the quality of government in Singapore is routinely listed at the top of a host of global rankings. That Singapore is already operating at the leading edge in many areas of governance means that it is no longer enough for government policymakers just to copy and adapt from elsewhere.

For many of the emergent issues that we have to deal with, Singapore will have to evolve its own strategies and approaches. To achieve real break-throughs, the government will have to depend more and more on its own innovations.

And as a result, the government will have to assume new levels of entrepreneurship with its attendant risks and uncertainties. A government that explores will also at times have to sacrifice some degree of efficiency in service of discovery. And it will need to become expert at conducting bounded experiments.

Indeed, the emergent, complex issues of the 21st century suggest the need for a new paradigm in governance — one that is Whole-of-Government, networked, innovative, exploratory and resilient in the way it confronts the challenges of our time, challenges rooted in complexity and accelerating change of the Anthropocene.

What is the appropriate model of governance for Singapore going forward? The coming years will see a growing need for *governance* — which requires collaboration across the public, private and people sectors — rather than *government* acting as the sole or dominant player.

Today, the government faces a myriad of complex public policy issues in which the trade-offs are much more difficult to make, because each could lead to unintended consequences and risks. Many of these public policy issues exceed the capacity of government working alone. Instead, they require the active contribution of private and people sectors. A government-centric approach focused on efficiency and productivity will likely give way to a broader approach that leverages on the collective capacity of non-government actors, in order to achieve results of higher public value and at a lower overall cost for society.

How government interacts with the private and the people sectors will in turn determine how big a role each of these sectors will play. It is often overlooked that the Singapore government has been a world leader in the engagement of the private sector. A succession of five economic reviews — the Economic Committee of 1986, the Committee on Singapore's Competitiveness of 1998, the Economic Review Committee of 2003, the Economic Strategies Committee of 2008, and most recently, the Committee on the Future Economy of 2016 — saw the public and private sectors coming together every few years to produce far-reaching policy recommendations for Singapore's long-term economic competitiveness.

Free Market *Versus* Market Intervention

A major factor that determines the size of our government has been our belief that free market forces should determine prices and economic outcomes. This is the approach that is the foundation of small government.

But in Singapore, faith in the market has not been uncritical or absolute. Instead, the government recognises that in certain cases, unfettered market forces can result in excessive volatility, negative externalities and under-provision of merit goods, like education, as well as public goods, like defence.

The economist Dani Rodrik outlined a framework that can be usefully applied to understanding how Singapore has chosen to blend the work of markets and the government:[17]

- First, the government has sought to *enable markets*. This includes ensuring rule of law, property rights, and public infrastructure — functions that most governments perform. In Singapore, enabling markets has

---

[17] Ravi Menon, "Markets and Government: Striking a Balance in Singapore," (speech, Singapore Economic Policy Forum, Grand Hyatt, Singapore, 22 October 2010), Economic Society of Singapore, http://ess.org.sg/Events/Files/2010/R_Menon_speech.pdf.

also included industrial policy and capability development, subjects of some controversy in policy circles around the world, especially among proponents of small government that believe in the *laissez-faire* approach.

- Second, the government has sought to *regulate markets*. This includes supervision of the financial sector, competition regulation, and taxation of negative externalities, such as high charges for car ownership and road usage, and sin taxes on alcohol and tobacco products — and maybe in future, taxes on sugary drinks. But a key feature of Singapore's approach has been the shift towards lighter regulation accompanied by risk-based supervision, most recently exemplified by the Monetary Authority of Singapore's FinTech regulatory sandbox.

- Third, the government has sought to *stabilise markets*. This is the bread-and-butter of macroeconomic management. Singapore's basic approach in monetary and fiscal policy is not far different from global practices. But its efforts to address asset price inflation and credit crises are interesting examples of targeted interventions that harness market forces.

- Fourth, the government has sought to *legitimise markets*. Globalisation, free trade, and open markets lead to significant dislocations. Some of the sharpest debates over the role of governments centre on this: To what extent should governments facilitate adjustments, redistribute incomes, or provide social safety nets, so as to maintain public support for market-oriented policies?

Engaging the People Sector

Complementing government and markets, is the role that society will play in tackling the great challenges and wicked problems of the 21st century.

A key part of this governance process will be growing mutual engagement between the public and people sectors. In his 2011 National Day Rally, Prime Minister Lee Hsien Loong underscored the importance of such engagement, pointing out that the nation needs to "harness our diverse views and ideas, put aside our personal interests and forge common goals."[18]

---

[18] Lee Hsien Loong, "Prime Minister Lee Hsien Loong's National Day Rally 2011 Speech (English)," (speech, National University of Singapore, 14 August 2011), Prime Minister's Office, http://www.pmo. gov.sg/newsroom/prime-minister-lee-hsien-loongs-national-day-rally-2011-speech-english.

This is especially important because people's expectations have changed — and are changing, continuously.

Maslow's Hierarchy

I think that there are a couple of reasons for this development. The first reason is that as government policies lead to improvements, the needs of the people change in tandem. This is explained by Maslow's hierarchy of needs. Maslow's proposition was that after the basic physiological needs of a person are met, more complex psychological needs would have to be fulfilled. At the top of this hierarchy of needs are the need for *self-actualisation*, which is to realise the individual's potential, and *transcendence*, which is helping others achieve self-actualisation.

So, if you accept this proposition, then after government has delivered on the basic needs of food, security, shelter, transport, and health, the expectations of the people are going to change, not in demanding more of the basic needs, but in fulfilling their more psychic needs in the upper reaches of Maslow's hierarchy, including social, emotional and self-actualisation needs.

The challenge for governments everywhere is that success in delivering the material goods of life — housing, food and so on — is no guarantee that it can be successful in delivering "the good life", however defined. I suppose the reverse is true as well, although it is hard to imagine the good life without the basic necessities of liveability.

Third-Generation Singaporeans

The second reason is what I term the *third generation effect*. Singapore is now 51 years old, and into its third generation of Singaporeans. The first generation of Singaporeans lived through the turbulence and uncertainties of Merger and Separation. The next generation started life on a firmer footing, but at the same time imbibed from their parents a sense of the vulnerabilities. But the third generation of Singaporeans have known only the affluence and success of Singapore. For them, the uncertainties of the 60s and 70s are abstractions from their school history books. When their grandparents speak of the turmoil and danger that they experienced, they shrug their shoulders because it is an experience outside theirs. Of course, they are hardly to blame for this, and they certainly need not apologise for it. Singapore's founding generation made the sacrifices so that their children and grandchildren would enjoy peace and prosperity.

And clearly, what persuaded their parents and grandparents will not wash with the third generation. But as long as we are all in this together — and I hope that they feel they are in this together — the hopes and dreams of our youth must also appreciate the tough realities that endure. By all means, dream, but dream with your eyes wide open. So, communicating to the third generation will require fresh arguments and different approaches.

People Empowerment

Citizens today feel empowered, because of the social media, and higher levels of educational achievement. Indeed, Singaporeans today are much better educated than their grandparents. In 1965, the cohort participation rate for university education was a miniscule 3 per cent. Today, it is 30 per cent.

The non-profit group, Ground-Up Initiative (GUI), points precisely to how attitudes are changing in Singapore. GUI operates a 26,000 m^2 "Kampung Kampus" space in Khatib, with the aim of reconnecting urbanites to the natural environment. The group's founder, Mr Tay Lai Hock, said:

> I think the top should set the example, but I also believe, you first and foremost, must take responsibility for your own life. Don't blame anybody. Don't blame the Government... I have a choice to decide that even though they have made this policy, I don't want to be a victim of their policies.[19]

The Bukit Brown Case Study

In 2011, the Land Transport Authority announced plans to construct a road that would cut through Bukit Brown, the oldest cemetery in Singapore. Heritage groups protested, while the government maintained its position on needing land in land-scarce Singapore.

---

[19] Bharati Jagdish, "Don't Blame the Govt; Take Ownership of Choices: Ground-Up Initiative's Tay Lai Hock," Channel NewsAsia, 9 July 2016, http://www.channelnewsasia.com/news/singapore/don-t-blame-the-govt-take-ownership-of-choices-ground-up-initiat-7903714.

When Bukit Brown Cemetery was placed on the World Monuments Watch in 2013, one member of the group All Things Bukit Brown said:

> I hope it shows that we are serious, that we want a seat at the table, just so we can present what we have heard from the community, what we have heard from the people who have encouraged us… you want development, but let's have a discussion, perhaps.[20]

The government has to deal with an electorate that feels empowered, demanding, and actively seeks participation. In this regard, Our Singapore Conversation, launched in 2013, signalled the government's commitment to listening to the people's views.

The Case of the Missing PM2.5

By looking at issues from the perspective of end-users — namely, the citizen — the government is able to design better policies than if they were to just use the usual top-down approach.

During the 2013 haze, experts had advised the government to consider releasing another indicator besides the Pollutant Standards Index (PSI) readings: the PM2.5 readings, which measure particles smaller than 2.5 microns. This is because PM2.5 particles greatly affect people with heart disease, as well as children and the elderly.

When the haze began, the government published the three-hour PSI readings and 24-hour PM2.5. But netizens and doctors pointed out that the PSI did not factor in PM2.5 readings as air quality indicators. Members of the public also expressed concern that the PSI values appeared different from what they had observed. Singaporeans even resorted to taking their own real-time air quality readings with commercial equipment.

The government said at first that it would be confusing for the public to have too many figures to read. But in the end, because of persistence of the public, the National Environment Agency began providing more information on PM2.5 and, from 20 June 2013, started publishing the PSI and PM2.5 figures hourly, six days after the haze began. Eventually, from 1 April 2014,

---

[20] Kirsten Han, "Singapore: The Fight to Save Bukit Brown," *The Diplomat*, 30 October 2013, http://thediplomat.com/2013/10/singapore-the-fight-to-save-bukit-brown/.

Singapore moved to an integrated air quality reporting index, with PM2.5 incorporated into the PSI as its sixth pollutant parameter.

Government With You

I have spent some time explaining how and why society in Singapore is evolving, and how government itself has to evolve in tandem. Put simply, it means a shift from the paternalistic and interventionist "government to you" and "government for you", to "government with you". The imperative is for government to move towards a collaborative approach to policy-making, and be prepared to connect, consult, and co-create with the people and the private sectors.

Order *Versus* Disorder

The bureaucratic propensity is to create order and consistency, both in the external environment and domestically. In Singapore, the inclination to manage extends even to our wildlife.

The recent case of chicken culling in Sin Ming is one example. Ms Natalia Huang, an ecologist at an environment consultancy Ecology Matters, recently suggested in *The Straits Times* that since Singapore is land-scarce, even regulating the number of cars on the road, wildlife should likewise be regulated.[21] With scientific research on how much space to allow wildlife density growth, we could ensure that wildlife in Singapore is sustainable.

Reducing Complexity *Versus* Catalysing Complexity

While governments and people try to reduce the complexity out there by coming up with all kinds of regulatory systems, there is a limit to how much order we can — or should — produce in a complex environment. It is both an aesthetic as well as an economic issue.

Literacy, political structures, levels of industrialisation, and per capita income, are conventional indicators of economic health. However,

---

[21] Natalia Huang, "Singapore Should Have Wildlife Control Down to a Science," *The Straits Times*, 22 February 2015, http://www.straitstimes.com/opinion/singapore-should-have-wildlife-control-down-to-a-science.

economists like Ricardo Hausmann, César Hidalgo, and Luciano Pietronero have suggested that the most important predictor of growth is economic complexity, or the diversity of products that an economy possesses.[22]

Countries with the most natural resources tend to have simple economies, as they do not produce unique goods. Thus, economies that are dependent on a particular kind of export — for example, oil or timber — may do well when demand for these products are high, but fail in the long run because they are not diversified enough and cannot compete in other sectors.

The ability to produce unique goods and services depends on the amount of "productive knowledge" in an economy. This is the kind of knowledge derived from experience and exposure to different sectors and domains of production. Invention and innovation occurs when these bits of productive knowledge are connected. Improvements to economic growth can be achieved either by harnessing existing capabilities in new combinations, or by accruing new capabilities to expand the productive potential of the country. It is an important outcome of economic complexity.

So, governance of a city state like Singapore is not all about reducing complexity. Far from it — instead, in some cases, it should catalyse complexity, by creating more networks to connect multiple economic domains.

The Rise, Fall, and Rise, of Boston

Harvard economist Professor Edward Glaeser tells of how Boston, in the 17th and 18th centuries, was the leading port in America.[23] It thrived as a conduit of goods between the old world and the new. But by the mid-18th century, Boston as a port had been eclipsed, first by Philadelphia, then by New York.

What saved Boston from the fate of other New England ports was a large population of Irish immigrants. By the late 19th century, Boston had transformed itself into a centre of manufacturing built on immigrant labour, and it prospered on the back of America's industrialisation.

But Boston's heady period of growth was over by 1920. Population growth slowed and even began to shrink after 1950. However, in the last

---

[22] César A. Hidalgo and Ricardo Hausmann, "The Building Blocks of Economic Complexity."
[23] Edward L. Glaeser, "Reinventing Boston: 1630–2003," *Journal of Economic Geography* 5, no. 2 (2005): 119–153.

two decades of the 20th century, Boston again re-invented itself, this time from an industrial city in decline into a high-tech, service-based economy. Its population grew rapidly between 1980 and 2000, reversing 50 years of stagnation and shrinkage.

Boston is now a centre of the information economy. Today, education is the dominant factor in Boston's economy. Boston ranks highly in its share of employees in managerial and professional jobs. Its top four export industries today are all skills-based: technology, finance, education, and healthcare.

Lessons From Boston

Using the lens of economic complexity, the Boston case shows us that the ability to re-orientate and create new value hinges on economic complexity. From its earliest days, Boston was never just a port. Artisans manufactured some of the goods traded on Bostonian ships. Boston had banks, brokers, and insurers from its seafaring days because shipping needed financial services. Education was always valued in the colony — Harvard University was founded in 1636 with government money.

Its rich, complex strengths and competencies enabled Boston to reach within itself to find new connections and value propositions. These enabled Boston to re-invent itself time and again when other more brittle, less economically complex cities like Detroit, which was heavily dependent on manufacturing — especially of automobiles — went into terminal decline.

Can Singapore rely on our position as a global transhipment hub, or will we have to confront the possibility, in the future, that changes in technology, logistics patterns, and geo-political shifts, that our pre-eminence as global port will decline? And then, like Boston, will we be able to reinvent ourselves?

Paralysis by Analysis *Versus* Acts of Faith

When a government becomes bogged down by the minutiae of day-to-day operations, the risk is that it will not be making the big decisions needed to take the country forward in a timely fashion. Arguably, the modern metropolis that is Singapore was itself an act of faith — in the people — an act of imagination and courage borne out of challenging circumstances.

Jurong Industrial Estate

Jurong Industrial Estate was the key to Dr Goh Keng Swee's plan to industrialise Singapore and drive economic growth, shifting the economy away from entrepôt trade towards manufacturing. In 1959, the newly elected People's Action Party confronted a huge challenge — sky-high unemployment estimated at 14 per cent or over 200,000 jobless people, and the population growing at around 4 per cent to boot.

Dr Goh's vision to transform the swamps, jungles and small fishing villages of Jurong into a modern industrial estate was based on Dr Albert Winsemius' report on Singapore's economic potential, which emphasised giving a big boost to manufacturing. Dr Winsemius was, of course, Singapore's long-time Dutch economic advisor.

But there were many sceptics. Jurong was seen by many to be a risky venture, given the absence in Singapore of any real track record in manufacturing, the choice of an area rural swamp land for the project, and the huge cost involved.

Dr Goh himself joked that if Jurong failed, it would go down in history as "Goh's folly".[24] Still, the government pressed on, with Dr Goh describing the project as "an act of faith in the people of Singapore".

By 1968, almost 300 factories had been built at Jurong, providing employment for 2,000 people. Jurong's big breakthrough came in 1968 when EDB persuaded Texas Instruments to visit Singapore, which then started up its plant in Jurong within 50 days of its decision to invest. It was an extraordinary vote of confidence in Jurong and in Singapore.

Dynamic governance in Singapore is an unending series of re-imaginings and reinventions. So, Jurong Lake District will be transformed into Singapore's second Central Business District. The KL-Singapore High Speed Rail Terminus will be located there. And Jurong will also be the site for the future Integrated Transport Hub, a new gateway to Singapore.

Tanjong Pagar Container Terminal

The Tanjong Pagar Container Terminal was also another early act of faith. In the 1970s, the shipping industry was enduring one of the most severe

---

[24] *The Straits Times*, "Some Who Thought Jurong was 'Goh's Folly'," 22 May 1970.

shipping crises ever experienced, affecting shipping companies with high investments in tankers and tramp or bulk ships.

Against this backdrop, Tanjong Pagar Container Terminal emerged as a potential solution. The country's shipping industry needed to exploit a growing market and a completely new transportation mode could help Singapore to remain competitive.

It was a calculated gamble that PSA took — under Mr Howe Yoon Chong's chairmanship, Singapore started building the region's first container port even before a single shipping line had committed to call at Tanjong Pagar. The terminal itself was constructed against the advice of professionals.

Though business was slow in the 1970s, container trade rose in the 1980s, giving Singapore a first-mover advantage, leading it to become the world's busiest container port in 1990. Today, Singapore is the second busiest container port in the world, and only one of two in the 30 million TEU class, after Shanghai.

Long-Term *Versus* Short Term

The point of this dialectic on governance is not to posit false binaries where there are none. There are no absolute "rights", especially not when the world is constantly changing. What the government needs to do is to prepare itself — and Singapore — for the black swans and disruptions that will surely surprise us in the future.

To achieve this, the government must put into proper perspective the pressing day-to-day concerns within the larger context of longer-term challenges and uncertainties.

The question you might wish to pose is, what is "the long view"? How far ahead can and should we really think? Some policy issues, such as demographics, the environment, and education, stretch out over many years. In contrast, government institutions are designed for four- to five-year electoral cycles. Even if we had the political will, do we really have the imagination to view and tackle challenges that lie beyond the life-time of the already-born citizen?

At the same time, we talk about making the future; but if we were to reframe it, is it not also the case that our actions in the present are "taking the future" away from unborn generations to come? Here I am thinking of our actions — or rather inaction — on a global basis with regard to climate change, for example.

This is a question of responsibility and trade-offs. On one hand, the current generation has a responsibility of stewardship, for example in steering Singapore to SG100 and beyond. However, in order to fulfil that duty of stewardship of the future, certain tough decisions have to be taken in the here and now. How much appetite is there really for long-term thinking in a society that is focused on the short term, dealing with the problems of the day, and "putting out fires" all the time?

This is why thinking about the future is an essential and yet delicate task for governments to foster — both as a matter of institutional processes and as a habit of thinking.

Singapore's success in managing its paradox has been achieved by a mixture of good government, good luck and a heavy dose of *kiasu-ism*. But Andy Grove, late CEO of Intel, once said, "Success breeds complacency. Complacency breeds failure. Only the paranoid survive."[25] This echoes something that Lee Kuan Yew himself once said:

What I fear is complacency. When things always become better, people tend to want more for less work.[26]

But, of course, too much paranoia can ultimately consume a society. Paranoia suggests always looking over your shoulder, always being driven by threats, rather than also looking out for opportunities. Paranoia, taken too far, can also lead to a loss of solidarity within society, leading to people viewing the world purely in zero-sum terms. What about being pulled forward by the *better angels of our nature*, instead of being chased by demons?

Thank you.

---

[25]Andrew S. Grove, quoted in William J. Baumol, Robert E. Litan, and Carl J. Schramm, *Good Capitalism, Bad Capitalism, and the Economics of Growth and Prosperity*, (New Haven: Yale University Press, 2007), 228.

[26]Lee Kuan Yew, "Summary of Speech by the Prime Minister at the 10th Anniversary Celebration of the Jalan Tenteram Community Centre," (speech, Jalan Tenteram Community Centre, Singapore, 27 June 1970), National Archives of Singapore, http://www.nas.gov.sg/archivesonline/data/pdfdoc/lky19700627.pdf.

Question-and-Answer Session
Moderated by Mr Chng Kai Fong

Chng Kai Fong (CKF): Thank you, Mr Ho. Just to give him some time to catch his breath, I thought I would begin by sharing a story about Mr Ho — at least, my own personal story.

This was about 10 years back or so, and he gave me a lot of grief then. He was then the Head of Civil Service. I was a young officer at the Ministry of Home Affairs, and my specific job was to plan for a flu pandemic. You know the implications of a flu pandemic, right? People catch the flu, tens of people will die. We thought all was well on the planning front, because my job was basically to work with the different agencies, the Ministry of National Development, Ministry of Social and Family Development, and all that. And then Mr Ho decided to throw a spanner in the works. He said, "This is all rubbish, you guys are not planning for the worst!" He referred to the Spanish Flu, where 100 million people died. And literally in Singapore, I think, by some records, 3,000 people died.

Mr Ho pooh-poohed all our work, and set up his own team of senior, high-level officials. He called it the "Blue Finch" and said, "You guys, challenge the current team in thinking about the scenario."

So my job doubled overnight because, in the daytime, I wrote papers planning for a flu pandemic and at night, I wrote papers debunking what his team was criticising us on. But I share this story with you to show you what kind of person he is. He is a person that makes you uncomfortable, but he is also someone who is not afraid to ask difficult questions, even though you have done a lot of work. And he practises what he preaches. This was at least 10 years ago, and he is saying the same thing right now.

We all know prophets have no honour in their hometown, and now that he is out of the public service, I hope that he is able to be more candid about what are some of the issues we have to think about.

So, just to kick off, I was really surprised by how Mr Ho ended this speech, because as a young civil servant, I would have expected an older civil servant to end on the note of Mr Lee Kuan Yew, which is that "you guys are too complacent, be careful, success breeds complacency, do not be complacent." But he ended completely differently. He said: "Perhaps the danger is that we could be too paranoid." And that is very surprising for me because I was expecting an older guy to say, "You guys have not eaten enough salt." So what I want to ask him is, in what areas in government today, or in Singapore today, do you think we are over-paranoid? And in what areas do you think perhaps, we are too complacent?

Peter Ho (PH): Well, luckily, when you reach my age — and it is not as if I am that old — but when you reach my age, your ability to recall all those events, which my younger friend has tried to recollect, are lost to me. So I cannot remember anything about what he said. If he attributes these to me, well and good, but I am in the happy position of being able to deny that I remember them.

Look, this whole business of complacency and paranoia — it is part of a spectrum, and I do not think we can run away from the fact. This is why the focus of this lecture was on the very precarious position that Singapore is in. We are unusual, and I hope the lecture brought out some of the unusual characteristics of Singapore, apart from the obvious things like we are a small country, a sovereign state, and how you survive as a sovereign state. You can compare yourself to other city states like Vatican City or Monaco, or to city economies like Hong Kong — they do not have to worry about the things we worry about. In fact, we are probably the only country that has to worry about the things we worry about. And that is to maintain our position as a sovereign city state for as long as we can.

This means we have to be worriers! I think we have to be worried all the time. But if we worry without hope, we will also be in big trouble, because if the only function of government is to worry, and they convey this sense of worry to the population, without at the same time exciting the population about the positive things that could happen in the future, we are going to have a lot of trouble.

In fact, this is not an advertisement for my next lecture, but my next lecture is going to be titled, "The Future: Governance, Unintended Consequences and the Redemption of Hope". I am going to talk about hope because it is very critical. This is not to say we abandon all this focus on worrying about things that could go wrong. But at the same time, it is part of the way we have survived. We have survived because there has been hope. And I would say the first generation of leadership gave a lot of hope to Singaporeans. We started with nothing but, somehow, we were lucky that we had leaders who gave us hope. Now the new generation of leaders must still give this hope. It is not as if we are off the treadmill.

CKF: If I can just push you on that, are there areas in which we are in danger of being over paranoid, that we have lost hope?

PH: No, in fact, my worry is the opposite. My worry is that we think that we have arrived, that we have started to succeed in a whole range of things. In fact, we have been very successful — I will not itemise them. But the big danger for us is not that we are too paranoid, but that we are not paranoid enough.

And what are the things that could upset the apple cart for Singapore? There are many things! I have mentioned the port as one example. I am not picking on the port, but I am familiar with the port, because I was the chairman of the Maritime and Port Authority many years ago. And right from day one, I asked: What happens when the trans-shipment model no longer works? Are we prepared for that day? Just because you are successful — you are the world's busiest port, you are the number two container port in the world, and you have become an international maritime centre, does not mean your position cannot be dislodged because of changing technologies. What happens if something replaces container traffic?

In fact, I remember just recently reading a very interesting study. This is about 3-D printing, or additive manufacturing. The study, I think done by PwC, PricewaterhouseCoopers, shows that something like 37 per cent of global container traffic will be affected once 3-D printing goes mainstream. And of course this same principle applies even to air cargo. Same problem. So disruptions are going to be everywhere. If you are not thinking about these things, and what could happen if things change — and things will change — then you are going to be caught, and you will have a lot of problems.

CKF: Thank you for that. Maybe just one more question before I open this to the floor, which is that you talked about how we need to shift from govern-ment to governance, and from government of you, for you, to government with you. Can you elaborate a little bit more on the structures we need? What are some of the new models of organisation that government needs to consider? I think you alluded to some of that in your previous lecture.

PH: I have already touched on something, which I think we tend to do rel-atively well, and that is in the economic arena, where the government has quite regularly and systematically found a way to engage the private sector. This is not just tokenism, where the government says, "Oh, I want to talk to you," and we talk to the private sector. All those economic review committees, which I touched on, are very serious efforts to get inputs from the private sector, and to take in those inputs, when reviewing whether the assumptions of economic policy need to be changed. And if they do, the government has shown that it is prepared to change. In that sense, there are no sacred cows.

Now, it is also very clear that, the area that the government is beginning to take more seriously is in engaging the people sector. This is a newer area. It is perhaps slightly more uncomfortable for the government, but I think the first major step was "Our Singapore Conversation". Of course, we are not going to have an Our Singapore Conversation every year or every few years. It is a huge undertaking. But that was a sign that government acknowledges that they have to engage the people sector, and in smaller ways, I think a lot of policies do require this early engagement.

It is not as if the man in the street does not understand that decisions have to be made, and that, sometimes, decisions will not meet with cheers all round. But I think what they want is, they want to be involved in the process, and that means government must engage them early, not late in the day. Part of the problem with Bukit Brown, if I may, was that the engagement came rather late in the day, when the plans kind of looked as if they were more or less firmed up. You can try to think of a future where you start talking about these plans much earlier on, before they are virtually signed, sealed and delivered.

CKF: Okay, great, let us open the floor for questions.

Participant: Peter, you started the lecture by saying that sovereign city states are exceptions, and you looked at history. What is your prediction of Singapore's continuity and survival as a sovereign city state, say 30 years, 50 years from now? Do you believe that Singapore will continue to prosper as one? What makes Singapore so special?

PH: Well, I am not really in the business of trying to make predictions. I have stated in all lectures, including this one, that prediction is one of the most hazardous things one could try to do. But I want to fall back on — they are not apple-for-apple comparisons, but the two examples I brought up, of Boston and Venice. Venice lasted almost 700 years, before it finally got absorbed. I think the Austrians took over Venice, and finally it got absorbed into the Italian state. But despite a lot of challenges along the way — the loss of special routes to the east, ceding to places like London and Amsterdam, Venice was still able to make its way in the world, and stayed a viable city state for 700 years. Boston is an example of a city that has prospered in spite of challenges. It is not a city state, but it is a city, and of course, you know in larger countries, cities come and go.

Now, what is common? One of the things that is common, apart from being small and reasonably self-contained, is the fact of good governance. Good governance is very critical. The Venice example is a case of good governance. They were very imaginative. In fact, many of the practices they adopted, including the willingness to bring in foreign talent, characterised Venice. Venice looked after its own defence, but also knew how to run a very nimble foreign policy, which meant it could somehow navigate through the challenges of being surrounded by a lot of big and rapacious neighbours. So that was Venice.

The example of Boston shows that you also have to make some decisions about what kind of economy you are. Because if you tend to have an economy based on a single product, you are going to have a lot of trouble. If you want to keep going, you have to be able to reinvent yourself all the time. In a way, Venice was a bit brittle, but it is still a miracle that they lasted so long. It was brittle because they were highly dependent on being at the top of one of the big trade routes. And when they ceded that position to the British and to the Dutch. That had a big impact on them, but they still stayed on for a long time.

So the short answer is, I think nobody knows what is going to happen to Singapore. But the whole purpose of making the presentation today is to show that you can look forward with some confidence — if you recognise the world for what it is. If you are prepared to make some of the hard decisions to keep going, then you will just keep on going like the Energizer bunny. But I do not know. I would say we have to be paranoid. But without hope, it is no use. They have to go in tandem. You have to be paranoid because paranoia helps you make hard decisions, and you have to make tough decisions. But tough decisions without hope — and hope is critical to bringing the whole system along with you — you cannot make it. This, in the end, boils down to good government and good governance, and good leadership.

Participant: How do you think the government can improve its effectiveness in communicating its policies and intentions to the people? Because at present, some policies may be a bit hard to understand for some people, myself included.

PH: The government has to focus a lot on how it communicates. We have very complex policies, whether it is CPF or whatever, and they are getting very complex because a lot of rules are attached to them. Communication itself is a non-trivial matter, and any government agency, which is responsible for rolling out these complicated policies needs to spend a lot of time thinking about how it is going to communicate them. If they do not think about it, and they only think about it as an afterthought, it will lead to a lot of confusion and some pushback.

This is also related to the point I made in response to an earlier question, which is, it is important that, when you are tackling some of these wicked problems and you need to have some buy-in. Communication is also about buy-in. You need to have early engagement to explain why this is an issue. You need to explain what the problems are, why there is no straightforward solution, why there has to be some kind of compromise, and why sometimes the decision may have to go against what some would like.

This whole process of communication is vital. I am not simply talking about communicating through tweets and things like that. I am talking about serious communication. Sometimes you have to go through townhall meetings and spend time on that. Tweets are not good enough when you are dealing with complex issues.

Participant: Earlier, you talked about how Singapore is successful because we adapt, not because we adopt. But now, that is no longer going to be sufficient. We need to innovate and create our own opportunities. For that to happen, what kind of culture does our society need to have, and how will we develop towards having that kind of culture?

PH: You have identified something that I feel quite strongly about. As you say, it is no longer just about adoption. It is about adaptation, but more importantly it is about innovation, because we are dealing with new types of problems. If other governments have not grappled with this kind of problem, we have to then deal with these problems and find our own way forward. But, and this is really the nub of the issue, I think it starts in government. How brave are the civil servants who are going to have to formulate innovative responses? How brave are they to try out something that is new, that has no real precedent? Think about it. It is possible to do that!

We have done this before. A case that springs to mind is the old area-licensing scheme, which morphed into the ERP. We were one of the first to do something on such a large and systematic scale. But that requires a certain courage and willingness to try something out. So it is not as if we do not have that kind of experience. The question is, is that instinct still deeply embedded in our system? I personally feel that sometimes, we tend to under-rate ourselves. The reality is, as a government, we are actually performing at the leading edge. We are actually doing very well. And there are many things that we do well on, which are a result of an innovative spirit. A lot of the people I used to interact with when I was still in service used to admire

Singapore, and I think they still do. We should not put ourselves down, and think we are not able to innovate. We can, and we should.

Participant: Nowadays there is an emergence of Mr Trump, and also the Philippines' Mr Duterte. Their way of communication is very carefree and simple. How would you see this emerging trend, of such leaders of major nations? Is it a reaction to changes in the people sectors, or is this simply them trying to be different from the previous administration, which may have been perceived as less successful by some?

PH: I think some of the developments we have seen, particularly in the last year, are the result of disappointment in the ability of governments to deliver the goods. So, a lot of people are very frustrated. They are even angry. They have lost their faith in the traditional form of governments, and are prepared to put a bet that, maybe other types of governments may do better. This is what we see in the form of more populist governments being elected, a rising form of nationalism, and this is partly a failure of governments. Governments have failed. They have failed to confront the issues, they have failed to communicate the issues, and they have failed to deliver on the solutions. When people lose faith in this kind of governments, they will put their bets on "snake oil" solutions. My personal view is that, in the end, they will be disappointed. But do we really have to go through that sort of pain? I think that is an unfortunate situation.

Now, in Singapore, you have to make a choice: what type of government do we want? Do we want a populist government? Do we want a government that tweets all the time, and changes its view on the turn of a dime? Or do you want issues to be discussed soberly, maturely, with the government working out the best possible solutions under the circumstances and with the resources they have? We all have to make this kind of choices. The people have spoken in other countries. They have made choices. I personally think that the choices they made were not very good ones, but they made those choices and they will have to live with them.

Likewise in Singapore, we have to decide what kind of government we want. And, as I said, the government itself has to evolve with the times. It is not that they need to indulge in populism or become more nationalist. But

I think it has recognised that people's expectations are changing, and it has to manage those expectations. If you cannot manage those expectations, it is no point talking about coming up with the best possible policy solutions, as you are not going to get the necessary support.

Participant: When the first generation of leaders took over, they were highly risk-taking and innovative about Jurong and those things. But it seems that we have gotten to the situation now where we have so much to lose, so we do not take any risks.

It is quite telling, Peter, that you mentioned that civil servants are no longer as risk-taking. But risk-taking, of the nature we are talking about and if you go back to our first generation, is done by politicians. If the first generation of leaders had left it to the civil servants then, I am not sure all the things that happened would have happened. When you talk about risk-taking, is it really about the civil servants, or is it higher than that?

PH: I think it is for the innovations, which are the big innovations, not small innovations. In fact in some ways I do not like the term "innovation", because it gives the impression of people innovating here, there, everywhere. But actually you are talking about the big transformations, the game-changers. Who is going to make them? That is not just a question of the top leadership being prepared to do it. It is also a question of whether the government, up and down the line, are prepared to make those changes. And of course you lose nothing by preserving the status quo in the short term.

But in the long term, it is going to lead to dysfunction and misalignment. And if you attended my last lecture, I spoke about Clayton Christensen, who wrote *The Innovator's Dilemma*. He identified the basic problem, the conundrum every successful organisation, whether you are a company or a government or a country, faces. Once you become successful, you are caught on the horns of a dilemma. On the one hand, you are trying to preserve your achievements, your successes. On the other hand, you know that there are all kinds of insurgents snapping at your heels, who are trying to dislodge you from your pole position. This is a dilemma. And all successful organisations and countries, I am afraid, are trapped on the horns of this dilemma.

This makes it very important that you have a certain humility — that just because you have succeeded, you are not necessarily going to feel confident that success is going to continue. Now, I spoke about this in my last lecture, and I mentioned the importance of taking a leaf out of Clayton Christensen's book, *The Innovator's Dilemma*, which is to create small disruptive organisations within the larger organisation, whose job it is to try out new things. These are what they call bounded experiments. They try things out, if they succeed, they succeed, then you proliferate, then you extend. If they fail, it is self-contained. But if you do not have this habit of trying new things out, then I am afraid that, in the long run, you lose that sharpness, which is vital to staying ahead of the game.

And I would say that this is not just a challenge for the top political leadership. It is also something for the government as a whole. I gave the example in my talk the last time. What did we do in MINDEF? We created the Future Systems Directorate, whose job it was to innovate. And on the backs of the innovation they did, we created the Third-Generation Singapore Armed Forces. You have to think of things like that. I am not saying it will work everywhere, but we will have to think of things like that. If you do not, we are in big trouble.

Participant: For the last 50 years, we have done a remarkable job, nothing short of a miracle. We have reclaimed land; even our water, which was initially very dicey. Now we are quite comfortable. In fact, we were so comfortable that in 2011 when one of the agreements with Malaysia stopped, we did not even feel it. We did not even know about it.

My question pertains to the future, because I understand part of the next lecture is about hope. But in very many ways, I feel hopeless, largely because the problems that have been solved. But the problems in the future seem to have hit what I consider the physical limitations. It is not mental; it is physical.

Take these three things. One, space. We have done a remarkable job with space, we were three hundred square kilometres, now we are seven hundred square kilometres, but how far more can you go? Currently we have five and a half million people, by 2030 we will have 6.9 million, and then what, 10 million? I mean, with five and a half million people, the roads are jammed, the MRTs are always crowded, etc. How far more can we go to solve these problems? Second is water. Can we get enough water anymore? There is a limit again. And the third problem is demography! As you all know, Singapore's largest problem now is that the people are getting older, and there are insufficient young people to support the old.

So these are all physical constraints and I cannot see us solving them in the next 50 years. Of course, I do not have to worry, I do not have that long to live, which is fantastic. But many other people will have to. Do you think Singapore might disappear as a sovereign state? Thank you.

PH: Well, first we should not be despondent, because the human race has shown a remarkable ability to innovate, and to come up with new solutions. Just to address a few of your points: first, if you say you would not be around, I am not so sure, because if we believe the data, a lot people who are here in this room today will live to be a hundred and beyond. Certainly, the students here with us in the audience, I think, are going to hit hundred and beyond. So you may still be around to see the effects of your sins of omission, or commission.

Having said that, let us just touch on a couple of things, because some of them I will touch on in my next lecture. Let us touch on this issue of space. What do you mean by space? Today, 12 per cent of the land area in Singapore is devoted to roads. How much of our land space is devoted to housing? 14 per cent! They are almost on par. When the government talks about this vision of a car-lite Singapore, it is as much to do with making sure that we have a sustainable transportation system, as it is about trying to reduce the amount of roads we have. That is one way. But there are other big solutions. The big solutions include underground space. Why must space always be what we see above ground? Of course, you can think of space by going upwards. And what about our sea space? I have been reading a book called *Seasteading*, about people who have got this vision of building cities at sea. And it is possible! The technology is available. A lot of the things we look at as absolute limitations today are actually being transformed because there are new technologies.

Likewise, you talked about water. I think we will continue to have to find new ways, and although we worry a lot about water, one of the most fortunate things is we are surrounded by the sea. So long as the sea is there, we have options. In fact, our problem is perhaps we have too much sea, because there are rising sea levels, then we will have more sea than we really need. That is a problem that we will continue to tackle. So never think of the future in discreet terms. You must think of the future as a continuum. There will be continuous challenges, and hopefully, if you have got the right mindset, if you are thinking about the problems, you can find innovative solutions. This is why hope is very critical.

CKF: Let me just sum up with a quote by F. Scott Fitzgerald, who wrote *The Great Gatsby*. It goes: "The test of a first-rate intelligence is the ability to hold two opposing ideas in the mind at the same time and still retain the ability to function." Tonight we have heard many opposing ideas, many paradoxes, encapsulated in Singapore, and it is the test of a first-rate intelligence. But I think many people do not know the sentence that comes after that quote, and I will leave that with you: "One should, for example, be able to see that things are hopeless, and yet be determined to make them otherwise." I think that is the spirit in which we end.

Lecture IV

THE FUTURE: GOVERNANCE, UNINTENDED CONSEQUENCES AND THE REDEMPTION OF HOPE

Governance and Vision

I n June 1819, soon after founding modern Singapore on behalf of the British East India Company, Sir Stamford Raffles wrote:

> *Our object is not territory but trade; a great commercial emporium and a fulcrum whence we may extend our influence politically as circumstances may hereafter require.*[1]

Professor Mary Turnbull, who wrote the definitive history of Singapore, explained that Raffles wanted to "ensure Singapore's prosperity as a great port, to abolish slavery and injustice, to devise a way of government giving 'the utmost possible freedom of trade and equal rights to all, with protection of property and person', and to make Singapore a beautiful and orderly city, the intellectual and educational centre of Southeast Asia."[2]

---

[1] BBC Radio 4, "Raffles," Episode 44 (16 February 2006), *This Sceptred Isle, Empire: A 90-Part History of the British Empire*, http://www.bbc.co.uk/radio4/history/empire/episodes/episode_44.shtml

[2] Constance Mary Turnbull, *A History of Modern Singapore, 1819–2005* (NUS Press, 2009), 38.

Given that Singapore in 1819 was truly a sleepy backwater with only about a thousand inhabitants, Raffles' was a remarkably bold vision, which in the words of Turnbull:

> … reflected the most advanced radical, intellectual, and humanitarian thinking of his day. The type of society he aspired to establish in Singapore was in many ways ahead of contemporary England or India. And he established in Singapore a free port following the principles of Adam Smith and laissez-faire at a time when Britain was still a protectionist country.[3]

While Raffles and his successors may have laid the foundation of this vision, it would be another century and a half before another figure started to loom as large in Singapore's history — Lee Kuan Yew — and who would give effect to Raffles' vision, and deliver much more.

Of course, the trajectory of modern Singapore did not follow a straight line. There were many twists and turns, shaped in large part by gigantic forces outside the control of the colonial government. But in the last 50 years, it was political will, combined with pragmatic policies, effective governance, sheer grit, and hard work of its people, and not a small dose of good luck, which gave Singapore the extraordinary chance to convert vision — not of Raffles, but of the founding fathers of sovereign Singapore — into reality.

The Law of Unintended Consequences

Since becoming independent, Singapore has taken a hard-headed approach to policy-making, unburdened by ideology, and driven by the stark imperative of survival. The government adopted a lean and efficient approach to public administration, involving the careful analysis of public policy issues, judicious use and adaptation of existing best practices, and strong government regulation. At the same time, it showed an exceptional willingness to eschew conventional wisdom and the politically correct, and instead to

---

[3] Ibid., 50.

adopt pragmatic solutions — and leaps of faith — to deal with the *wicked problems* of the day.

Arguably, this approach could define good government and effective policy-making. But it is not a prophylaxis against the Law of Unintended Consequences. Governments — and public opinion — ignore the power of this law at their peril. Because of complexity, every government will sooner or later have to face the unintended — or unforeseen — consequences of its decisions. This is because in a complex world, conditions and assumptions that underpin policies and plans change over time, and that presupposes that the assumptions were even correct in the first instance. This leads to policies and plans having effects that are unanticipated or unintended, and outcomes that cannot be easily predicted. Of course, there are other reasons for unintended consequences, including sheer stupidity, blind spots, and other cognitive failures.

The Great Sparrow Campaign

A famous illustration of this law is the Great Sparrow Campaign, sometimes referred to as the Four Pests Campaign. During the Great Leap Forward, Mao Zedong launched an initiative to get rid of rats, flies, mosquitoes and sparrows — the eponymous four pests. Sparrows were considered pests because they fed on grain. So, Mao ordered the culling of sparrows. But nobody then seemed to have realised that sparrows not only feed on grain, but also eat locusts as an avian delicacy. By culling the sparrows, a delicate natural balance was upset, and soon there were not enough birds left to eat the locusts. As a result, locust swarms took over the countryside, devouring entire crop fields in their path, resulting in starvation, and contributing to the Great Chinese Famine.

Singapore's Population Policy

Singapore has not been immune to the Law of Unintended Consequences. Like many other developing countries, Singapore's population growth in the early years was high. In 1965, Singapore's total fertility rate, or TFR, stood at 4.66. The birth rate was 29.5 per thousand people. The concern then was that Singapore's population, which stood at 1.8 million in 1965, would climb to an unmanageable five million people by 2000. Like many other governments around the world, Singapore's was fearful of the potential Malthusian impact of high population growth, and so the government acted decisively to slow it down.

The government began a campaign to encourage smaller families. In 1966, the Singapore Family Planning and Population Board (SFPPB) was established, and the government launched the National Family Planning and Population Programme with the key public message of a "small family". In 1972, the government began its phenomenally successful "Stop at Two" campaign. Within three years, the birth rate had plunged from 23.1 to 17.7 in 1975, falling even beyond the target of 18.0 per thousand.

But the low birth rate soon turned into a cause for concern. This unintended over-correction arose in part because the policy was implemented ahead of developments in Singapore that have since been found to correlate with low birth rates — such as higher education and employment opportunities for women, and rapid poverty reduction and income growth. In effect, Singapore became a developed country in demographic terms, well before it became one in the economic sense.

Lessons of Human Nature

Social policies are particularly susceptible to the Law of Unintended Consequences, as human behaviour and societal changes are often shaped by deep, hidden and inter-connected forces that — because of complexity — might not be fully apparent for years.

This is where governments often run into the limitations of conventional policy levers. Public policies are aimed at changing overt human behaviour, such as imposing fines to deter littering. But they are often unable to tackle and shape its deeper aspects. For example, the government's Productivity and Innovation Credit scheme,[4] or PIC, that was meant to incentivise businesses to raise productivity and boost innovation, was also extensively "gamed", or abused, if you will, eroding the scheme's impact.

---

[4] The Productivity and Innovation Credit (PIC), under the Inland Revenue Authority of Singapore, allows businesses to enjoy 400 per cent tax deductions up to $400,000, or 60 per cent cash pay outs up to $100,000, for investments in innovation and productivity improvements.

Furthermore, decision-making in government is constrained by cognitive limitations which define our human nature. This is because of what Nobel economist Herbert Simon called "bounded rationality".[5] The rationality of an individual is constrained by the information that he has and the finite time he has to make a decision.

This challenge is accentuated in a hierarchy, including government. The decision-maker at the top receives all the information and makes the decisions. But because of bottlenecks caused by bounded rationality, the decision-maker is either surprised, with all his cognitive synapses saturated, or he lacks sufficient bandwidth to comprehend the full scope of the problem. This means that the decision-maker cannot possibly make a fully rational and optimal choice. Instead he will very often choose a course of action that "satisfices" — it is somewhat acceptable, but not optimal.

This means that our human nature renders decision-making an imperfect process — one that, even in the best of circumstances, does not lead to the optimal choice but to one that is only reasonable. Taking into account the challenges of complexity and the Law of Unintended Consequences, it leads to the depressing conclusion that government policies and plans cannot always be right, and certainly not for all time.

But this does not mean that we should sit on our hands in the face of such problems. Instead, we should approach such matters with a huge dose of humility, be prepared to shift course, and maintain an open mind. Having unintended outcomes does not mean that the policy was flawed in the first instance, or should not have been implemented. But it does mean that governments must be willing to change tack or even to reverse course if the policy appears to be drifting off course. Running pilots and experiments would also help.

The larger point here is that translations from policy intent to content and then to outcome are often not straightforward. When things go wrong, as they often do, how do we respond? Do we just look for someone to blame, or do we work to solve the problem? A blame-seeking culture can be both destructive as well as unproductive. It might satisfy a human impulse to hold someone accountable, but it certainly does not solve the problem.

---

[5] Herbert A. Simon, *Models of Man: Social and Rational* (New York: John Wiley and Sons, 1957).

The Future is Unknowable

"The past is a foreign country; they do things differently there."[6] This elegant and elegiac opening line in L. P. Hartley's 1953 novel, *The Go-Between*, is probably better remembered than the novel itself. It speaks to the essential reality of human existence that things are changing and moving forward, rather than staying still.

Understanding the future is hard. It has yet to unfold or come into being. The great financier J. P. Morgan[7] was once asked what the market would do. His learned reply was, "It will fluctuate."

We can guess what the future may be, but we face the same challenge as when we try to understand a foreign country — we cannot help but project our implicit assumptions. In thinking about the future, too often we take up one change that we think is powerful and important, and leave everything else as it is. So, we end up with a view of the future that is essentially an extrapolation of today.

This is because of an inherent linearity in our causal reasoning. There is plenty of research in cognitive psychology that show that we struggle to understand non-linear relationships, and tend instead to think in straight lines. We assume that there is proportionality between cause and effect — that is, big causes will have big consequences, and small causes only produce small consequences. This linearity often means that planners and policy-makers focus on the major forces in the social, economic, technological, political, and environmental spheres.

But some future states of the world are difficult to anticipate because they emerge out of developments that we may have overlooked, or because of developments that we know about, but whose interactions generate unforeseen outcomes.

High-tech "gurus" often confidently predict the "next big thing" on the basis of straight-line guesses or extensions of existing trends. But history has shown us that the way future technologies will interact with one another — and with users — has an emergent property, and is not always predictable from previous developments.

---

[6] Leslie Poles Hartley, *The Go-Between* (London: Hamish Hamilton, 1953), 1.
[7] Jean Strouse, *Morgan: American Financier* (New York: Random House, 1999), 11.

Instead, it is important to consider the world in all its dimensions — not just in politics and economics, but also society, culture, community, technology, and the marketplace.

I recall vividly a meeting with Chris Anderson, the former editor-in-chief of *WIRED* magazine. He told me that the almost all of the magazine's editors were liberal arts graduates, and not Science, Technology, Engineering and Mathematics, or STEM, graduates. The reason for this was that the liberal arts graduates were found to be best able to connect the dots, linking technology trends with social currents in a way that those schooled in single, discrete disciplines could not. The insight I drew from this is that in order to thrive in a complex future, we will need to manifest and match that complexity in our mix of backgrounds, skills, ideas, and perspectives.

Who Are We?

One common assumption when thinking about the future is that "we are who we are". But in that future, we would be changed, too. Our interests, habits, experiences, and expectations would be different. There is much that changes slowly in human society. Our cultural underpinnings are some of the slowest things of all to change, but even culture changes. And the further out we go, the more that future will be a truly foreign country.

During Our Singapore Conversation, Singaporeans discussed their hopes and concerns about the future. But they mostly took their Singaporean identity as a given. Reflecting on the process, Minister Heng Swee Keat said:

> We realised and learnt just how diverse individuals and groups are in our society and yet how much we share and value in common as Singaporeans.[8]

Similarly, when the Urban Redevelopment Authority develops the Concept Plan for land use over the next four or five decades, it assumes implicitly that our current identity as a nation state in a city, on an island, will continue.

---

[8] Heng Swee Keat, "Working Towards Our Aspirations," in REACH, *Reflections of Our Singapore Conversation* (2013), 4.

Changing Identity

Yet identity can and does change. Just in the past century, Singapore had gone from being a Crown Colony in the British Empire, to *Syonan-to*, or "Light of the South", during the Japanese Occupation, to being part of Malaysia, and then the Republic of Singapore after Separation.

This is more than about changing names. It is also about how people see their lives and their sense of place. Many saw themselves as sojourners in Singapore when it was a Crown Colony, not citizens. But many of them and their descendants today see themselves as citizens — Singaporeans in Singapore, their home. So, the answer to the seemingly innocuous question — "Who are we?" — may change in the future, opening new situations and new options.

Indeed, long-lived successful companies often reinvent and redefine their identities. One might argue that this process is part of what helps them survive, that reinvention of identity builds resilience and *antifragility*, qualities that I touched on in my second lecture. When Steve Jobs and Steve Wozniak incorporated Apple Computer Inc. in 1977, the company only made personal computers. Thirty years later, in 2007, Apple renamed itself Apple Inc. It was a subtle but important acknowledgement of the changes that Apple had undergone. By then, Apple was making more than Macs — it also made iPods and the iPhone. It would later go on to make the iPad and develop the App Store.

Singapore as a Charter City

In an op-ed published in *The Straits Times* in January this year, Benjamen Gussen, a law lecturer at the University of Southern Queensland, gave an example of how Singapore could redefine its identity.[9] It could provide the infrastructure for a charter city in Australia, which would attract Singaporeans and migrants from other parts of Australia. In a charter city, the governing system is defined by its own charter document, rather than by state or national laws. In Gussen's view, this would offer Singapore and Singaporeans space

---

[9] Benjamin Gussen, "A Proposal for a Singaporean 'Charter City' in Australia," *The Straits Times*, 24 January 2017, http://www.straitstimes.com/opinion/a-proposal-for-a-singaporean-charter-city-in-australia.

beyond current physical and political boundaries. The charter city would be a global city that would also boost growth in Australia.

To be sure, only a few charter cities have sprung up. Paul Romer, the current World Bank Chief Economist who champions the idea, cites Shenzhen and Hong Kong as examples of charter cities.[10] But even if this specific idea may not gain much traction, it raises this possibility — that the *idea* of Singapore need not be confined to this small island.

Virtual Singapore

Imagine what identity would mean in a future where people live not just in the physical world, but through Virtual Reality (VR) and Augmented Reality (AR), also live in alternate worlds — part real, part virtual.

Is this science fiction? Maybe not. The propensity to spend a large part of our waking hours in a virtual world is already here. A Nielsen report last year revealed that the average American adult spends 10 hours 39 minutes staring at a screen each day.[11] Last year, people the world over, including in Singapore, witnessed the astonishing phenomenon of pedestrians walking about blindly — smartphone zombies — oblivious to the danger of traffic whizzing around them, totally absorbed in tracking down Pokémon in the AR game, *Pokémon Go*.

In March this year, Elon Musk, the CEO of Tesla and SpaceX, launched a brain-computer interface start-up called Neuralink, which is developing a "neural lace" technology that would involve "implanting tiny brain electrodes that may one day upload and download thoughts." He later spoke of "some high bandwidth interface to the brain… that helps achieve a symbiosis between human and machine intelligence."[12]

In such a world, what would identity mean? If the individual inhabits virtual worlds for much of his waking hours, connected through avatars on his smart devices, or linked through some version of Elon Musk's "neural

[10] Paul Romer, "Interview on Urbanisation, Charter Cities and Growth Theory," (interview transcript, interview with *iMoney Magazine*, 29 April 2015), https://paulromer.net/tag/charter-cities/.

[11] Nielsen, "Total Audience Report: Q1 2016," http://www.nielsen.com/us/en/insights/reports/2016/the-total-audience-report-q1-2016.html.

[12] Elon Musk, "A Conversation with Elon Musk," (speech, World Government Summit 2017, Dubai, 13 February 2017).

lace" technology, then where is his emotional and psychological centre of gravity? In the old days, the emotional space that the individual occupied coincided exactly with the physical space that he lived in. But in future, this alignment may be disrupted by advances in digital and even neurological technologies. Do we embrace this future, as a nation, accepting then that the notion of national identity may change, or at least become more ambiguous? Or should we repudiate it? The answer lies in our fundamental attitudes to the future.

What Can We Influence?

By population and geography, Singapore is truly small. We see ourselves as price-takers.

Because we are a small country, we often speak as if the future were a car speeding towards us — we can swerve, or we can run backward. But we can scarcely control the car. In my second lecture, I spoke about how Singapore, in its short history, has experienced change not as a *velocity*, but as an *acceleration*. The world changes and affects us. We adapt or perish.

Prime Minister Lee Hsien Loong captured this view in a speech at the Singapore Institute of Technology in October 2016:

> *We know the world is changing. You cannot predict how. You cannot predict when. But you must gird ourselves for whatever might happen, and adapt to new conditions as they come up.*[13]

The Innovator's Dilemma

There are good reasons for this view. Examples abound of successful organisations that fail. Some failed to discern changes or failed to change. One example is Nokia, a classic case study in Clayton Christensen's *Innovator's Dilemma*.[14] Nokia was the market leader when Apple introduced the iPhone

---

[13] Lee Hsien Loong, "PM Lee Hsien Loong at the Singapore Institute of Technology Dialogue with SITizens 2016," (speech, Singapore Institute of Technology, 24 October 2016), Prime Minister's Office, http://www.pmo.gov.sg/newsroom/pm-lee-hsien-loong-singapore-institute-technology-dialogue-sitizens-2016.

[14] The "innovator's dilemma" is that faced by leaders who focus too much on improving their existing products and neglect to safeguard their company's future through disruptive innovation.

in 2007. It was an early adopter and driver of 2G technology, a world leader in both supply chain management as well as global brand-building. It was the first handset manufacturer to target the bottom two-thirds of the global income pyramid. Nokia was among the first to understand the importance of ease of use, design, and of mobile phones as lifestyle products. As a result, half the smartphones sold around the world then were made by Nokia.

But by 2010, this figure had fallen to one-third. Nokia failed to develop the software and smartphones to compete with Apple and Google. It had failed to see that the mobile Internet was a practical option, and it could not find a credible response to the iPhone and Android OS. It even rejected the development of a Nokia App Store. It was the beginning of the end. Eventually, Nokia threw in the towel and sold its mobile phone business to Microsoft in 2013.

Influencing the Future

We need to consider how we can influence change — how technology develops and impacts us, and how markets are created and change. There are good reasons to focus on structural changes. History is emergent. Among the many possible paths that history could have taken, the interaction of structural factors and human agency led it down one path.

If we relaxed the constraints of Singapore as a price-taker, what new options to reinvent ourselves could we consider?

One view of technology is that it will advance and affect us — but as an external and often frightening force. We say that technologies, such as Artificial Intelligence and robotics, will "disrupt jobs". Jobs will be automated, so we must prepare ourselves. Robots may be alienating, so we must mitigate these risks.

The sentiment that technology is beyond human control and frightful finds expression in art. Victor Frankenstein creates a sentient being who kills people. In the 2004 film, *I, Robot*, robots try to take over the world. In the 2015 film, *Ex Machina*, the humanoid robot, Ava, outwits her creator and escapes into the world, leaving viewers to imagine the consequences.

Yet, people and societies do shape technology. Japan is investing in robotics, to shape how the field advances. Rather than build cold metallic objects to disrupt jobs and society, it wants to integrate robots in everyday life, as if they were *social beings*. The Japanese have taken robots and made them soft and cuddly — turning "objects" into "social beings". And perhaps not surprisingly, because in the Shinto religion, even inanimate objects can have a soul.

Japan's "New Robot Strategy" of 2015 envisages a "robot barrier-free society", where robots teach foreign languages, set tables and help the elderly walk and go out. Rather than develop virtual assistants — say along the lines of Apple's Siri or Amazon's Alexa — the Japanese firm Gatebox has built Azuma Hikari. She is more virtual companion than assistant — a theme explored in the 2013 film, *Her*. Azuma comes "alive" as a holograph, advises her master to take an umbrella when there are prospects of rain, and nags him to come home soon during the day.

Another area where it is easy to accept things as a given is markets. One view of markets is that businesses need to adapt. So, if the demand for business class seats weakens, companies such as Singapore Airlines may want to diversify into budget airlines. If the demand for fossil fuel weakens amid climate change, oil majors such as Shell may want to diversify into renewables.

Luxembourg

Yet people and societies can also create and shape markets — even small societies. Fewer than 600,000 people live in Luxembourg. Ten times as many people live in Singapore. Yet Luxembourg is creating a market for harnessing resources in space. In November 2016, it introduced a bill to let companies own resources, such as platinum, obtained from space. It has set aside €200 million to support asteroid-mining companies. It has attracted two US firms, Planetary Resources and Deep Space Industries, to set up offices in Luxembourg as part of efforts to nurture this new market out of the Grand Duchy.

Lest these efforts to create a market seem like a moon shot, Luxembourg has experience; it founded and invested in Société Européenne des Satellites (SES) in 1985, launching its own space industry. Today, SES is one of the largest satellite operators in the world.

The case against technological or market determinism is not an argument for ignoring realities — our small population, our small land mass, or the region in which we live. It is an argument for striking a balance between adapting to the world and shaping it. Our Smart Nation efforts offer us a chance not just to adopt technology, but also to shape it to serve national priorities — an idea I described in my second lecture — and to create markets for integrating technology, governance, and what people need or want.

Where Are We?

Thomas Friedman has described our world as "flat".[15] Everything is linked and connected to everything else. Globalisation and advances in transportation and communication technologies have put nations, peoples, and enterprises in touch with one another as never before.

But there is another metaphor used by Richard Florida, who argues that the world is "spiky",[16] not flat. His argument is that higher value-added activities are densely concentrated and clustered in hubs — what he calls the mega-regions of the world. These hubs and connectors of the world have superseded nation states as "natural economic units".

Singapore as a Hub in the Global Network

Singapore is part of a flat world. But it is also part of a spiky world. Singapore is today a global and regional hub of many things. Since Raffles' time, Singapore has been an important trading and maritime hub between East and West. Singapore is also a major connector in international aviation, and a key node in the global financial system.

But Singapore's position as a hub is neither unassailable nor preordained. History shows that hubs come and go. Malacca used to be the centre of the spice trade in Southeast Asia. Venice was the centre of East-West trade throughout the Middle Ages. Rangoon, now Yangon, was the aviation hub of Southeast Asia before 1962.

Is it important that we are a hub, a peak among the valleys in a spiky world? Simply defined, hubs are the exceptionally well-linked nodes in a *network*. Throughout history, hubs have been the main engines of economic growth and development. Network theory provides insights to explain why

---

[15] Thomas L. Friedman, *The World is Flat: A Brief History of The Twenty-First Century* (London: Macmillan, 2005).

[16] Richard Florida, "The World is Spiky: Globalization Has Changed the Economic Playing Field, But Hasn't Levelled it," *Atlantic Monthly* 296, no. 3 (October 2005): 48.

hubs acquire wealth more easily than other nodes in a network. The world's economic geography is dominated by hubs, which are the focal points of opportunity, growth, and innovation. Firms locate to where skills, capabilities, and markets cluster. Capital flows to where returns are greatest, and highly skilled talent move to where opportunities lie.

This was what happened in Venice, which I touched on in my third lecture. As a city primarily concerned with trade and commerce, Venice was not a major producer of artistic and scientific talent. Instead, it imported talent — *foreign talent*. Attracted to Venice's wealth and position as an intermediary between the East and West, artists and scientists flocked to the city during the Renaissance, making it a vibrant hub of culture, ideas and scientific knowledge. Today, Singapore's approach to attracting top talent to boost the R&D sector echoes the Venetian example.

Today's economic geography is also dominated by hubs. They are defined as places that claim significant economic capacity, substantial innovative activity, and highly skilled talent. Singapore is one of these hubs. Contrary to Tom Friedman's flat world thesis, the existence of hubs reflects the reality that both economic activity and innovation are highly concentrated, and become more so as one moves up the economic ladder. Economic activity continues to cluster around highly connected hubs. In this spiky world, the tallest peaks — the hubs — will continue to flourish and grow higher, while the valleys will languish. In other words, the rich hubs at the peaks get richer, while the poor in the valleys stay poor. This is the *power law*. This means that in a network, there will always be just a few densely connected nodes — or the hubs — and many more nodes with only a few links.

The Hub in a Future Networked World

But even then, the nature of hubs will change. What will a hub look like in future? It would be fatal to assume that the density of connections that Singapore has today and the centrality that it enjoys in today's networks — whether in air transportation, maritime, or other networks — are permanent.

When we think of our place in the world, we often think about physical geography. The British set up a free port in Singapore because it is located on the trade route between India and China. The epithet "Little Red Dot" is today a badge of pride for Singapore and Singaporeans. Singapore is represented on maps as a red dot. Our sense of geography connects with our feeling of vulnerability and advantage.

Yet this sense of geography is based on a particular kind of map. Modern maps relate one place to another in terms of longitudes, latitudes and borders. They look at the world from a bird's eye view.

But this has not been the only way of viewing one's place in the world, as Benedict Anderson, the historian and political scientist, writes in his book on nationalism, *Imagined Communities*.[17] Ancient Thailand had two kinds of maps. It had *diagrammatic guides*, which helped people make war or set sail, using distances measured in terms of marching and sailing times. It also had *cosmographic maps*, which guided people on less tangible, even spiritual journeys. Singapore is much less adept at this second type of cartography.

One could say that we represent our place in the world in maps to serve our needs. If we relaxed our constraints of physical geography, and imagined new maps that transcend physical territory, what new opportunities might open up? And how can these new opportunities help us to reconceptualise our map of the world? The charts in Parag Khanna's *Connectography*,[18] for example, point to the growing influence of data flows in shaping our "map" of the world.

The Impact of Digital Technologies

In the recent past, Singapore tried to overcome its small physical size by tapping into space abroad — such as Suzhou Industrial Park, Iskandar Malaysia, and Batam, Bintan and Karimun. It was, and is, a network strategy with Singapore as the hub.

But, new digital technologies will create new and different networks with their own hubs and connectors. If 3-D printing or additive manufacturing successfully transitions to large-scale manufacturing, it could significantly reduce global shipping activity, negatively affecting all aspects of the port and shipping industry, including the transhipment market that Singapore's position as a global hub port is based. In one study, PwC

[17] Benedict Anderson, *Imagined Communities: Reflections on the Origin and Spread of Nationalism* (Brooklyn: Verso Books, 2006).

[18] Parag Khanna, *Connectography: Mapping the Global Network Revolution* (London: Weidenfeld & Nicolson, 2016).

estimates that up to 37 per cent of the ocean container business is at risk because of 3-D printing.[19]

So, whether we will continue to be a hub in the networks that emerge in future will depend not just on our capabilities, but also on our ability to seize early mover advantages, and on how quickly we create and attract links to Singapore in the new networks that emerge.

If such changes occur, we may need new maps to complement old ones. I would like to examine two ways in which our needs may be changing.

Rethinking Borders

First, we often think of economic competitiveness based on nations, demarcated by borders. One nation is more competitive than another in a particular sector. This view made sense when nations traded goods — whichever had a comparative advantage in making a product ought to make it, to the benefit of all.

The economist Richard Baldwin, however, says that the *flows of know-how* have grown more important in the past two or three decades, as communications technology improved, and enabled coordination from a distance.

The worker in Ho Chi Minh City, Vietnam, or Zhengzhou, China may not know how to design, manufacture and market a product. But the multinational corporation, or MNC, does. By training the worker and his manager, the MNC taps into cheaper workers and land. Consciously or unconsciously, it adds them to global value chains. "The contours of industrial competitiveness are now increasingly defined by the outlines of international production networks rather than the boundaries of nations," Baldwin writes.[20]

This may mean working more closely with major companies and cities that are part of the production networks, whether to develop new products and services, orchestrate these networks or even shape where and how these networks develop.

---

[19] Andrew Tipping, Andrew Schmal, and Frederick Duiven, "2015 Commercial Transportation Trends," *Pricewaterhouse Coopers*, 2015, http://www.strategyand.pwc.com/global/home/what-we-think/industry-perspectives/perspectives/2015-commercial-transportation-trends.

[20] Richard Baldwin, *The Great Convergence* (Massachusetts: Harvard University Press, 2016), 6.

Baldwin speculates that improvements in communications will enable other flows — even those of high-touch services, such as seeing a counsellor, or working with a physiotherapist — across national borders. Remote medicine, where patients interact with doctors in a different location, is already practised. Today, Rio Tinto manages its mining operations remotely. In the future, digital platforms can to tap into labour based abroad, without even setting up a Singapore-supported industrial park abroad. Such platforms, like Konsus, already exist. Konsus matches high-end independent contractors or freelancers with projects, including when the freelancer and the project client are based in different places. If cross-border supply of services increases, Singaporeans may be able to work with co-workers and clients based abroad, as if they were physically present in Singapore.

Singapore under the British thrived because of its status as a free port. In contrast, Jakarta — then known as Batavia — languished under the Dutch because of onerous restrictions placed on traders and the Dutch policy of controlling and taxing trade. Being well connected and plugged into dense networks confers far more advantage than efforts to monopolise production or control access to resources. The Portuguese in Malacca, and later the Dutch, sought to control the spice trade by collecting monopolistic rent in Malacca and by limiting access to the spice-producing islands. While this generated short-term profit, it backfired in the long-term as merchants sought to by-pass Malacca for less restrictive ports. The British, in contrast, maximised their commercial power by linking up its empire with ocean cables, the telegraph system, railways and canals, with the Suez Canal being the most important. They created the first truly global market and controlled the sea lanes with just "five keys" that were said to lock up the world — Singapore, the Cape of Africa, Alexandria — which commanded access to the Suez, Gibraltar, and Dover.

The basic approach is to ensure open access and maximum connectivity. Just as Sir Stamford Raffles made Singapore a free port in 1819, welcoming traders from any country, Singapore in 2017 could welcome data from any country — a free data port. It could allow data centres in Singapore to hold data governed by the laws of another country, as if it were stored in the source country. This would anchor the data in Singapore, allowing local-based companies to harness insights from data. Such rethinking of borders will grow in importance in our increasingly digitised and data-driven world.

Rethinking Connectivity

Second, the flows of data will accelerate. It is not just the data that we generate on WeChat and Facebook. Machines will communicate more with each other. Complexity economist Brian Arthur describes machine-machine communication as a "huge interconnected root system."[21] These interactions and interdependencies take place underground, out of sight, but enable actions that we care about. Mobile phones communicate with GPS satellites to pinpoint our location so that Grab drivers can find us, without our being aware that this communication is taking place.

If the movement of data from one IP address to another will matter more in the future, nations may need to reconsider how to plug themselves into these flows, given the possibility that countries will protect the sovereignty of data. Some countries are already mandating that data about their citizens is stored locally. Others are setting rules on the transfer of data across borders.

Today, Singapore manages its relations with other states, through the diplomacy and the conduct of foreign policy. In the future, it will need to manage relations with a wider range of entities — with digital conglomerates, with cities, and even with other countries — in the digital space. This will not be without precedent.

Denmark is reported to be creating the position of technology or digital ambassador, that some have dubbed the "Silicon Valley Ambassador" — in order to better engage digital firms, such as Apple, Google and Facebook. This is almost as if technology was its own country, unlike the present and certainly the past.

Although the role is still being fleshed out, Danish Foreign Minister Anders Samuelsen explained the need for greater engagement by citing recent investments in Denmark by Apple and Facebook, increasing data usage, and attendant issues of privacy, and "fake news". For Singapore, such an approach would build on our earlier efforts to partner other cities and sub-national regions to plug them into international production networks.

---

[21] W. Brian Arthur, "The Second Economy," *McKinsey Quarterly,* October 2011, http://www.mckinsey.com/business-functions/strategy-and-corporate-finance/our-insights/the-second-economy.

Reinventing Singapore as a Global Hub

Changes in technology, trade routes and geopolitics can gradually diminish a city's or a country's hub position. Hub positions are not invulnerable despite the many advantages that incumbency confers. The commercial power of Venice declined after Christopher Columbus' discovery of the New World and Vasco de Gama's discovery of a sea route to the Orient. The example of Venice suggests that global hubs like Singapore need to diversify their offerings and constantly reinvent themselves to remain relevant.

Estonia — A Harbinger of the Future

From medieval and Renaissance Venice, let us turn to a much more modern example. Estonia is a Baltic state of 1.3 million people. It borders Russia, making it all the more diminutive. It is ageing, like Singapore, and even older; 19 per cent of its population was aged 65 years and above in 2015, higher than the 12 per cent in Singapore.

Despite its size, location and age — or perhaps because of these factors — Estonia has been turning itself into a digital society. At birth, the doctor puts the Estonian baby's details into the medical records, and so his digital identity is born. That digital identity now allows an Estonian to sign private contracts, access public services and databases, pay taxes, and vote. In the 2015 parliamentary election, 30 per cent of votes were cast over the Internet. By cutting trips to public offices and banks, for example, the digital society is estimated to save Estonia 2 per cent of GDP yearly.

Beyond the digital society, Estonia is also re-creating itself as a "virtual nation". First, it is trying to back up its computers and databases, so that the Estonian digital society can continue to function, even when cyber-attacks or physical attacks occur. In 2007, online banking was crippled and emergency services almost disabled in a massive *Distributed Denial of Service* (DDOS) cyber-attack on Estonia. This took place amidst a row with Russia over the relocation of a Soviet-era statue. To build robustness, Estonia is now experimenting with "digital embassies", where data is stored on servers in its embassies abroad. It is also developing ways to migrate data to commercial servers, such as those hosted by Microsoft, as back-up in the event that cyber-attacks take place.

Second, Estonia introduced e-residency in 2014. You may be Indian, South African or Singaporean. You may live abroad. If you become an e-resident of Estonia, you can use some of the digital services available to Estonian citizens, such as setting up an Estonia-based company. E-residency helps Estonia generate business activity for Estonian companies, from independent contractors to small companies with clients worldwide. More than 18,000 people have since become e-residents.

Estonia hints at how nations could redefine their identities, and what it means to be a nation, in a digital era. Benedict Anderson, whom I cited earlier, argues that a nation is an imagined community. E-residency may one day build another "Estonia" — an imagined community beyond borders and time zones. Digital embassies are about ensuring the survival of a country's way of life, beyond physical borders.

"The concept of a country has changed," says Taavi Kotka, Estonia's former chief information officer who led the e-residency initiative. "Land is so *yesterday*. It doesn't matter where you physically live or operate. That is how the game will change."[22]

Is Kotka right? Or will geography and territory have the final say? Perhaps the question should not be cast in such binary terms. Singapore is already simultaneously a nation state and global city. To consider Singapore also as an extra-territorialised entity, expanding the concept of our reality to encompass abstract bits and data flows, merely reinforces the paradox that we already are.

Where Next?

It was Singapore's great fortune to have had two remarkable visionaries in its short history of two centuries — Stamford Raffles, the founder of modern Singapore, and late Minister Mentor Lee Kuan Yew, the father of independent Singapore.

The question is whether Singapore should tempt fate, and leave it to luck that another great man will emerge to lead the nation to even greater

---

[22] Mathew Reynolds, "'Land is so Yesterday': e-Residents and 'Digital Embassies' Could Replace Country Borders," *Wired*, 17 October 2016. http://www.wired.co.uk/article/taavi-kotka-estonian-government.

glory? Or whether we should create the conditions that will allow Singapore to extend its exceptionalism for as long as possible into the future?

I am of course inclined to the latter, not just because I believe that passivity opens us to greater turbulence, and increases the likelihood of strategic shock. It is also because I believe that action creates hope. Hope is the fuel that energises society, but hope also needs action to make vision become reality. As Bill Willingham wrote in the *Fables* series, "Hope isn't destiny. Left passive, it's nothing more than disappointment deferred."[23]

Our founding fathers' grand vision and great hopes for Singapore were always accompanied by action. This is the difference between hope and paranoia — the latter has a crippling capacity to cause all action to be for naught, while the former propels reasonable, thought-out action with measured optimism.

The central question that is posed in this evening's lecture is whether Singapore is merely a price-taker, or whether it has the ability to influence and alter the factors that shape the future?

A thread running through all these four lectures — and this evening's in particular — is a hopeful view that even small city states can influence, shape, and even create, not just markets, but also their operating environment. It is a belief in this view that hope can be redeemed for even a little red dot like Singapore.

As a parting shot, let me outline two reasons for this belief. First, I do not want to trivialise Singapore's very real constraints. But these very constraints are our opportunities. Resource constraints matter more to us because we are small. We also have less room for systematic policy error in a world that is increasingly VUCA. But it is precisely our smallness that gives us agility, the ability to course-correct, and to iterate with more freedom and dexterity, than much larger entities. We have greater ease of coordination, to actualise the Whole-of-Nation approaches that I mentioned in my first lecture, since we can actually galvanise society within our small space. We have greater ease of implementation, and great ability to test, iterate, experiment and prototype, because we do so within limited geographical bounds. And as a small state, we have greater ability to

---

[23] Bill Willingham, *Super Team, Fables: Volume 16* (New York: Vertigo, 2011), 125.

course-correct if we happen to embark on policy at scale that turns out to have been wrong or misguided.

Second, we should remember that responding to complexity, uncertainty and accelerating change are not alien to us. It is in our very DNA as a country, and rooted in our origins both as a seaport founded by Raffles and well as a nation led by Late Minister Mentor Lee Kuan Yew and the other founding fathers. No one expected us to survive but we did. We defied rules, expectations, stereotypes and existing categorisations when we eschewed import substitution, courted MNCs and embarked on multicultural meritocracy when most of our neighbours were mercantilist and communalist. Both Goh Keng Swee's vision of a thriving open economy and S Rajaratnam's vision of being Singaporean by choice and conviction were audacious, reflecting a unique brand of *gung-ho* political entrepreneurship. My belief in the redemption of hope should not be seen as something new to Singapore. It is within each of us, and with a little effort we can reclaim it.

Of course, there are conditions attached. Prime Minister Lee Hsien Loong alluded to one of them when he spoke of his wish for a sense of "divine discontent",[24] which I take to mean never being satisfied, never being complacent that we have arrived.

Of course, it is hard to change the identities that we are familiar with — who we are, where we are, and what is within influence. Yet, changing identities is part of what it means to grow. You are not the same person that you were a decade ago, and hopefully you are the better for it. The winds of change provide an opportunity for us to reinvent ourselves.

We need courage and imagination. Courage to change the identities with which we have grown comfortable with, to rewrite the stories that we tell ourselves about ourselves, and imagination to come up with different identities. We should not feel that our success in future is derived from what we are today. If we can achieve such courage and imagination, then there is a basis to hope for a better future that is yet to exist.

This courage and confidence to embrace changes and opportunities together as a nation, rests on our sense of shared agency, values, and destiny — a shared future. A key source of Singapore's strength has always

---

[24] Lee Hsien Loong, "National Day Rally 2016 Speech."

been our people's trust in fair competition and just reward for effort and achievements, compassion for the unfortunate, and a restless yearning for continuous progress. The points on trust and compassion bear emphasising. This has to be carefully fostered by the leadership because, without it, it would have been impossible for our leaders to forge consensus on far-reaching policies and tough trade-offs between different priorities, interests, and groups.

From this interplay between internal hope and external forces of change, combined with vision and good governance, the future — our future — will emerge. As the 13th century Persian poet and scholar, Rumi, memorably wrote, "The garden of the world has no limits, except in your mind."[25]

Thank you.

---

[25] Rumi, quoted in Wayne W Dyer, *Inspiration: Your Ultimate Calling*, (Carlsbad: Hay House, 2006), 62.

Question-and-Answer Session
Moderated by Ms Chua Mui Hoong

Chua Mui Hoong (CMH): Thanks, Peter, it was a very invigorating lecture. Thank you, ladies and gentlemen, for being here tonight. I think many of us know Peter as a deep thinker, but maybe not so many of us know that he is also a very kind person who makes time for all kinds of people. I have known Peter on and off over the years as a journalist, and I remember, even when I was a young reporter, he was always very generous with his ideas and his time. I interviewed him for a book on the civil service when he was Permanent Secretary, and he gave me a lot of inputs. I am also most grateful to him because, two years ago, when *The Straits Times* commissioned a series of articles on SG50 — and of course we had to look to SG100, 50 years down the road, Peter was very generous in giving his ideas, and linking me up with his contacts. This is just my way of explaining why I agreed to overcome my usual reticence at public speaking, to agree to be here tonight.

So now I will just exercise my prerogative as moderator to ask the first question. I was very much taken, Peter, by your idea of imagined communities. I also liked your reference to the article on charter cities — not just because it had come out in *The Straits Times*, and I had edited it. It is an idea that has come up when I talk to several people, that maybe even the whole idea of nationhood and sovereignty is a constraint for Singapore's future. What do you think of that, and do you have any ideas in terms of what kind of arrangement or confederation might work for Singapore? Is sovereignty a constraint?

Peter Ho (PH): I think if you follow the thread of my reasoning, what Singapore is going to be in the future has to emerge out of a conversation and consensus within the society. So we make the future as we think we want it to be; and whether we are prepared to contemplate something like a charter city, or to do things like Estonia, creating an e-residency scheme, embracing, in a way, new networks, is something which we have to agree on. It is not something the government itself can mandate. It is not going to happen that way. It has got to be a consensus that we are at an inflexion point in our history. There are huge challenges and new global forces forcing change, and that we need a big conversation in Singapore on what we want to do in this period of great change.

Again, I have to link this back to my three previous lectures. The point that I was trying to make is that this change is irreversible. There is no point wishing we could go back to the good old days, because the good old days are gone forever. There is a new future being created, and we have to decide what kind of role we want to play in this future. What I wanted to say in this final lecture is that there are opportunities. Rather than seeing all the challenges as constraints, we should see things as a source of opportunity. And we have some advantages because we are small and we are nimble. So we can decide, and we can decide to move if we want to. If we had worried about constraints, I think Singapore would not be where we are today.

Participant: With regard to what you mentioned about the law of unintended consequences, what are your thoughts in relation to the upcoming presidential elections? The next question is, last week, I was fantasising with an old primary school mate. We were talking about how Singapore could possibly expand to Mars, and work with Elon Musk. Maybe one of these days, in the distant future, Majulah Singapura can be sung on Mars?

PH: Well, first, the point I was making about the law of unintended consequences is not to say that the policy on presidency is going to lead to unintended consequences. It might — on the other hand, it might not. That is not the issue. The basic issue about the law of unintended consequences is that, whenever we make a policy decision — and this connects to complexity, bounded rationality, and some of the other issues I have raised, we cannot be sure that the outcomes are going to be what we had planned for. And then, what happens? Do we start blaming people? Or do we say, there is a problem here? We started out with the best of intentions, but it looks as if there are certain things we had missed out. And therefore we either need to reverse course, or modify the policy. That is the point.

CMH: You can always change the law.

PH: And you can change the law, indeed, precisely. Regarding fantasies, I have nothing against fantasies. It is great that we have fantasies. But the point about fantasies is, which fantasies are we going to translate into action? If you want to raise the Singapore flag and sing Majulah Singapura on Mars — I think you cannot, because there is no atmosphere there, so the sound cannot be heard, but if you could, then okay, if the society wants to do it, then let us go in to see how we can do it.

Our small size actually has never been an impediment for us to influence major factors that some think are already predetermined. They are not! Many of the things we have done have actually been sheer acts of political will, combined with a certain doggedness, if you will. We do have that ability in us, and we have got a track record, otherwise we would not be where we are today.

Participant: How can Singapore strengthen our social system, such as by implementing the universal basic income, to prepare this country for the increasing amount of unemployment, which will be slowly happening around the world due to this wave of automation?

PH: Well, first point is, it is very important that we are not necessarily seduced by what other people do or what other people argue. So this idea of universal basic wage is in itself an issue that needs to be discussed, but it is not necessarily the solution. We are not trying to solve the world's problems; we solve our own problems. This, I think, speaks to the importance of having the Whole-of-Nation approach. You must have a conversation, decide on what the big issues are and which we need to worry about. If it is

"Do we need to provide basic wage for everybody?" — well, we can discuss that. But is that the big issue?

Let us go back to some of the themes in my four lectures. One theme is that things are changing very fast, and if we are not prepared to change, we will be left behind. When I talk about things changing very fast, I am not talking about velocity, I am talking about acceleration. We are at this unique juncture in history where things are accelerating, and we need to set aside past practices which seemed to have worked well for us, but which may not work well in the future. Now, if that means we have to contemplate radically new ideas, well, we should do so! But this is the acme of good leadership: how do you bring the people along with you? I think that requires an ability to converse and talk about these issues.

CMH: This lecture is being streamed live on Facebook so we have people watching us — hello, our online viewers! Here is a question from one of our viewers. The future of Singapore is actually quite old, considering our ageing population. How will this phenomenon shape public policy? Are we ready for this future?

PH: I think this is a huge issue — our demographic profile is ageing, and at some point we will begin to look like Japan today. The question for us is, what kind of solutions will we have, to address these issues regarding an ageing population profile. One is, how do you give people who are older a meaningful life, people who are going to live for much longer periods. Today, we say the average life expectancy is 83. In fact, many of the people here in this room are going to live to a hundred! It is a moving goalpost. So people who are going to age, how are you going to give them a meaningful life? How are you going to look after them? Where is the support, the financial support going to come from? These are big challenges.

Then you have other challenges in this kind of profile. Where are the young people who will provide the energy to energise the economy, to propel the country with new ideas, who are prepared to try new things out? These are very important challenges. The first society, which is confronting this in a very real way, is Japan. Japan has all the challenges of an ageing society, and an ageing society that lives very long, although I understand that the

Koreans are about to live longer than the Japanese. But it is the same thing. They are all living very long. How are they doing it? They know they have to keep the economy vigorous. So they have got to get young people out into the economy. It means they cannot depend only on young people to look after the old people. That is why I think their drive into robotics, Artificial Intelligence, is all a very interesting indicator of some of the possibilities for us in the future. But it is something we have to worry a lot about.

Participant: My question relates to the future of governance and politics. Different governments bring along different perceptions about the future, and if the political landscape in Singapore becomes a two-party pendulum, with one displacing the other every general election, would the civil service be able to withstand this constant fluctuation? There is a lot of talk about the need for the civil service to be adaptable and flexible. It is easy to say that, but it is hard and sometimes painful.

PH: My previous lectures had touched on this issue. The nature of government itself is changing, and has to change, in the light of how society is changing. What seemed to have worked very well for Singapore in our first 50 years, I think, has to give way to a more collaborative form of governance. It is not so much a debate over whether it is a one-party, two-party, or a three-party system, or you have one revolving door, and you always have the loyal opposition. That is not the debate. The critical debate is, what is the relationship between the government, the people sector, and the private sector? Unlike in the past, especially in the people sector, they now have a voice, which they did not have before. That voice is partly because of good education, but also comes from having access to social media, which we have discovered governments cannot ignore. Like it or not, the opinion of a group of people will be very loud, amplified by social media.

In a way, the form of governance, as opposed to government, is going to involve a lot more collaboration between the people and the private sectors, and the government. And that means, in a way, not just consultation, but also some willingness on the part of the government — and I do not know how they are going to do it — to extricate themselves from certain areas of policy and planning, where they currently play a very dominant role in.

Of course, governments should continue to be responsible for defence, and fortunately, outside of government, you cannot decide on defence policy, but I think in a lot of other things, government can leave it to the people and the private sectors to have a greater say.

Participant: How does one evaluate the performance of the futures thinkers that you talk about? Considering that it is not possible to distinguish between situations that have been avoided, and what would not have happened otherwise.

PH: The short answer is: the job of the futures thinker is not to predict the future. So, there is no way you can assess somebody who is preparing for the future on the basis of whether he got his "predictions" right or wrong. It is whether he has an ability to look at all the factors, and say, in a considered way, how he thinks those factors are going to influence how we are today, and how those factors can be harnessed to shape the future. It is not to predict the future.

Participant: I just want to build on the last comment you made about how the government has got to give space to the people and the private sector, and engage them more. And you are right, certainly not in defence policy but in other areas. Therefore, the obvious follow-up question is, how does Singapore create more space for alternative voices, dissident voices — voices that say things that are clearly outside the box, outside the formulas that we have used, that were probably rubbish in the last 50 years, but may actually work in the next 50 years. How do we change, in a sense, that political chemistry of the society that allows such voices to emerge?

PH: This is the kind of question you should be posing to the political leadership. But let me attempt to answer the question anyway. I believe, going forward, the government is going to realise that they have no choice but to open up and to listen to what the people are saying. I think a lot of the frictions we see today are because we have not yet gotten as comfortable with this kind of conversation on the social side. We are more comfortable with having this kind of open and frank dialogue on the economic side, but not on the social side. It is very new to us.

Looking at the way trends are developing, it is very clear that, first, the electorate is far better informed. They do their homework. Those that are serious — and if they do their homework, and if they can provide an alternative model — I see no reason why the government should not listen to them. I think the problem will come when the people just lash out, and look for somebody to blame. Then that leads to a very antagonistic type of relationship. But it means that the nature of policy-making itself will have to change. How do you make decisions? Do you make decisions only through the channel of civil servants writing policy papers, which then go up to Cabinet, Cabinet decides and, if necessary, the issue goes up to Parliament? Or do you have a process which starts much earlier, in which you have a process of consultation, dialogue, with all the different stakeholders. That is messier, and takes a lot more time. You are going to get some left-field views expressed, some ideas that are un-implementable — that is inevitable — but should we avoid this kind of thing?

My view is, in the future, we cannot avoid it. So, we have to move down that road. But then the leadership also needs to have a broader view of what decision-making is, and the people sector, in particular, also needs to know that this would require them to take a responsible approach.

Participant: Although you say that we are small and it is an advantage to us, to look forward and to give us hope, I cannot help but look at some of the recent issues where we had challenges. The first thing has been to create new entities. Rather than look to existing government set-ups to amalgamate them, to flatten them, I see more and more agencies. I retired in 2005 from government, and I remember that we had over 30 agencies then. Recently, we won a tender, where we were asked to support more than 100 agencies.

So, my question is, do we need 100 agencies on this small island? And then each agency has seven to nine layers of management structures. For those that need to take advantage of innovation, you have to be flattened. Look at Microsoft, look at Apple. But somehow we leave it to the traditional way; there are seven, eight, nine layers, even for agencies that need to innovate.

PH: This could be the subject of another IPS-Nathan Lecture Series. I have studied organisations for a very long time, and I think there is always a propensity, within any kind of bureaucracy, to create more and more arms and legs, and add more and more layers. Somehow, I think that they cannot help it. It takes a conscious effort to scrub it down to what is optimally required.

Unfortunately, there is always a justification for why you need this agency or that statutory board, that Ministry, and these are in and of themselves, you could say, perfectly justifiable. The question is: Are they serving the function that they set out to do? Or do they become bureaucratic impediments? That is very critical. This is a question that can only be answered by the leaders of these organisations. Do they just insert themselves into the system instead of facilitating decision-making and getting better outcomes, and become frictions in the system, slowing everything down?

So again you have to remember, in Singapore, no matter how good the government is, there is always a bell curve. There will be certain things that are most critical. Make sure you have the right people in charge of those critical areas — the people who have the ability to cut through red tape, who have the ability to cut the Gordian knot if necessary, to get things done, just to get the kind of outcome the government wants. The rest, well, they just continue as per normal. This is a reality of any kind of human organisation.

CMH: So do you think there are too many agencies in Singapore, which I think is at the heart of the question?

PH: I was always an advocate of making sure that we have a reasonable number of agencies, but we should be very careful when we add more agencies, and by agencies I mean things like statutory boards. I do not follow this in a great deal of detail today, but if you think that there are many more agencies than there were a few years ago, then it must be the case. But then the question is, are they doing their job properly?

CMH: A Facebook viewer asks, "History tends to recycle itself. In the future, do you foresee us getting involved or sandwiched again in any form of regional power competition? What principles should we adopt to survive?"

PH: We have to remember that we are going to be a little red dot in a much larger region of great diversity, and not always peaceful, sometimes quarrelsome. I think in this kind of world, you only make your way forward if you are strong, not necessarily strong in terms of size, but if you have an effective defence system. That means effective deterrence, a strong foreign policy, a very adept foreign policy. Lastly, you must be economically successful. If you are not, you cannot assert yourself. That is the reality. So, the fact that we have been successful economically has given us the basis to develop a strong defence capability, having a pragmatic as well as a very agile foreign policy has also given us the strength to manoeuvre in a very complex world.

CMH: Here is a question from another Facebook viewer. What do you think of the scholarship system in Singapore, which has led to many government leaders being scholars, who are in danger of groupthink, as well as being from a homogenous demographic? Is it something that needs to change, and change quickly?

PH: It is very important for the people who serve in government, the decision-makers, not to be cut from the same bolt of cloth. That is not to say that the scholarship system is bad. In fact, the scholarship system is a very important route for us to get talent into government. But the question is whether we should be much broader in reaching out to people who do not necessarily conform to a particular stereotype of what a good civil servant should be like.

And to give some credit to the government and the Public Service Commission, in recent years, they actually have deliberately looked at a person not just because he is good academically or because he comes from a particular junior college. Instead, they look at the whole person. So, this effort to diversify is, I think, taking place.

Participant: I would like to ask about the education of the students, because they are technically the future of our country. In your insightful lecture today, you mentioned Yale-NUS students, and the kind of liberal arts programmes that are very forward-looking. Would you encourage the students of Singapore today to go towards more of these kinds of generalised degrees, or not necessarily even a degree, towards a more generalised kind of education, rather than a specialised stream of thinking?

PH: Well, this will be a source of a lot of debate in future, but we need to develop a greater ability for our graduates from our school system to take an inter-disciplinary view of things. Solving our complex problems in the future cannot depend only on just the person being an excellent economist. He must have insight into how society works, just like having a technical solution is not going to be good enough. You have to think about what the social aspects are, what the economic aspects are.

So, this is one strength of the Yale-NUS liberal arts education, which is much more broad-based. They look at problems not from the perspective of a single discipline, but from a more broad-based view. Interestingly enough, this is not the only one in Singapore. The other one is the Singapore University of Technology and Design. And remember that that is about the design approach, whereby you solve problems holistically. That means you do not just bring to bear your knowledge of say, architecture, your knowledge of say, engineering. You look at other angles, and that is the whole essence of what it takes to operate in a complex world, where you have a lot of wicked problems, where there is no single factor that is necessarily the determinant of that problem. You have to look at things holistically.

So, I would say, an indicator of what the future brings is going to be seen in places like SUTD and Yale-NUS. That is not to say you should not study Physics and all of that, but you still have to have that broader view.

Participant: This is on the issue of the public, whether people are more active and more vocal. If I am at home, I spend about 10 hours on Facebook; I have 5,000 friends — the maximum you can have. Most of my friends are foreigners. You see, the Malaysians are very vocal. Even on WhatsApp, they are very vocal. But here, I see, people are very docile. Very passive. The fear factor is still working. Whenever I post something, I cannot sleep at night, thinking whether someone is going to take me away. So the issue is how to give more people confidence.

Just imagine today, I was watching BBC and CNN News. They were talking about the sacking of Comey, the FBI Director. By accident I switched on to Channel NewsAsia. It was plain! There was nothing analytical, nothing intellectual on the sacking. It was just plain sailing. The setting must be done by the government for people to be more vocal, for people to be given more space to articulate. The people here are intelligent! They are not stupid, you know. But the space is not there.

PH: Well, first, I would challenge your view that Singaporeans are not vocal. I think when they need to, they express themselves. The question we have to ask ourselves is, do we want to be a society that is always confrontational, where every issue is an issue of confrontation, or are we much more of a society where we say there are problems, and we say we try to solve the problems? I do not think it is necessarily a bad sign if our people only make noise on the big issues, and are relatively quiet on other issues. Why do you want to quarrel over every issue? You will get exhausted. I get tired just following what is going on in the US. If you are in the US, and you are a citizen of the US, you will be exhausted. The first hundred days is over, and they are still going on and on.

So, you really have to ask yourself what kind of society you want. And I would not jump to a conclusion that this society is docile. In fact, I have an opposite view on this, which is that they choose the battles they want to fight. I think that is the kind of thinking society you want, rather than a society where we fight over every issue that comes up.

Participant: You spoke about imagined communities and e-citizenship, and the question that came to my mind, that probably concerns Singaporeans is, how do you see National Service evolving? Just now, we spoke about how we will live to be a hundred. Do you see a reservist being called back even at 50? Our constitution allows for women to serve, to be conscripted, if there is a requirement, and I recall, we said there was no operational requirement. So in the next 50 years, this issue of rootedness and serving the nation, especially in defence, what would it look like?

PH: I recall having addressed this issue in one of the previous lectures, but let me just say very briefly that National Service has an obvious function, which is the defence of Singapore, which is vital for so long as we conceive of Singapore as an independent sovereign nation. And even with imagined communities, which I talked about, the physical Singapore is still important, so you still need some form of SAF. You still need some form of National Service.

But there will always be a perpetual tension between the desires of having a good and effective SAF through National Service, and other desires, which include being more of a global city and a more international hub, which will always put the two competing requirements into play. In each period of our history, we have to find the right answer, and right now, the right answer is, we must not compromise on defence, because we are going through a very difficult time. You think about other countries which have gotten rid of National Service or reduced National Service, I think it is the Swedish who are bringing back military service because the strategic situation has changed. So, circumstances change, and you have to make your decision at that point of time. I am not copping out, I am just describing how decisions have to be made, and there are no easy answers.

CMH: Thanks for all your questions, ladies and gentlemen, and thanks, Peter.

BIBLIOGRAPHY

Adler, Bill. *The Churchill Wit*. Coward-McCann: New York, 1965.

Anderson, Benedict. *Imagined Communities: Reflections on the Origin and Spread of Nationalism*. Brooklyn: Verso Books, 2006.

Anderson, Philip W. "More is Different." *Science* 177, no. 4047 (1972): 393–396.

Arthur, W. Brian. "The Second Economy." *McKinsey Quarterly*, October 2011. Accessed 16 June 2017. http://www.mckinsey.com/business-functions/strategy-and-corporate-finance/our-insights/the-second-economy.

Baldwin, Richard. *The Great Convergence*. Massachusetts: Harvard University Press, 2016.

Baumol, William J., Robert E. Litan, and Carl J. Schramm. *Good Capitalism, Bad Capitalism, and the Economics of Growth and Prosperity*. New Haven: Yale University Press, 2007.

BBC Radio 4. "Raffles," Episode 44 (16 February 2006). *This Sceptred Isle, Empire: A 90-Part History of the British Empire*. Accessed 15 June 2017. http://www.bbc.co.uk/radio4/history/empire/episodes/episode_44.shtml.

Beck, Ulrich. "Muslim Societies and the Western World Can No Longer Be Considered to Be Separate Entities." *Deutschland Journal*, 15 September 2009. Accessed 6 June 2017. https://en.qantara.de/content/ulrich-beck-muslim-societies-and-the-western-world-can-no-longer-be-considered-to-be.

Borsuk, Richard, and Reginald Chua. "Singapore Strains Relations with Indonesia's President." *The Asian Wall Street Journal*, 4 August 1998.

Chan, Heng Chee. "The PAP and the Structuring of the Political System." In *Management of Success: The Moulding of Modern Singapore*, edited by Kernial Singh Sandhu and Paul Wheatley, 70–89. Singapore: Institute of Southeast Asian Studies, 1989.

Christensen, Clayton M. *The Innovator's Dilemma: When New Technologies Cause Great Firms to Fail*. Boston, Mass: Harvard Business School Press, 1997.

Chui, Glenda. "Unified Theory is Getting Closer, Hawking Predicts." *San Jose Mercury News*, 23 January 2000.

Collins, James Daniel. *The Mind of Kierkegaard*. Princeton, NJ: Princeton University Press, 1953.

Diamond, Jared. *Collapse: How Societies Choose to Fail or Succeed*. New York: Viking, 2005.

Dyer, Wayne W. *Inspiration: Your Ultimate Calling*. Carlsbad: Hay House, 2006.

Eggers, William D., and Stephen Goldsmith, "Networked Government." *Government Executive*, June 2003. The Manhattan Institute for Policy Research. Accessed 6 June 2017. https://www.manhattan-institute.org/pdf/gov_exec_6-03.pdf.

Fisher, Herbert Albert Laurens. *A History of Europe*. London: Eyre and Spottiswoode, 1935.

Florida, Richard. "The World is Spiky: Globalization has Changed the Economic Playing Field, But Hasn't Levelled it." *Atlantic Monthly* 296, no. 3 (2005): 48–51.

Friedman, Thomas L. *Thank You for Being Late: An Optimist's Guide to Thriving in the Age of Accelerations*. First ed. New York: Farrar, Straus and Giroux, 2016.

Friedman, Thomas L. *The World is Flat: A Brief History of the Twenty-First Century*. London: Macmillan, 2005.

Furr, Nathan. "How Failure Taught Edison to Repeatedly Innovate." Accessed 8 June 2017. https://www.forbes.com/sites/nathanfurr/2011/06/09/how-failure-taught-edison-to-repeatedly-innovate/#4d69ed9365e9.

Gigerenzer, Gerd. *Risk Savvy: How to Make Good Decisions*. London: Allen Lane, 2014.

Glaeser, Edward L. "Reinventing Boston: 1630–2003." *Journal of Economic Geography* 5, no. 2 (2005): 119–153.

Goh, Chok Tong. "Transcript of Singapore Prime Minister Goh Chok Tong's Interview with Mr David Bottomley, Correspondent, BBC". Interview, The Instana, Singapore, 21 April 2003. National Archives of Singapore. Accessed 8 June 2017. http://www.nas.gov.sg/archivesonline/speeches/view-html?filename=2003042201.htm.

Gussen, Benjamin. "A Proposal for a Singaporean 'Charter City' in Australia." *The Straits Times*, 24 January 2017. Accessed 15 June 2017. http://www.straitstimes. com/opinion/a-proposal-for-a-singaporean-charter-city-in-australia.

Han, Kirsten. "Singapore: The Fight to Save Bukit Brown." *The Diplomat*, 30 October 2013. Accessed 14 June 2017. http://thediplomat.com/2013/10/singapore-the-fight-to-save-bukit-brown/.

Hartley, Leslie Poles. *The Go-Between*. London: Hamish Hamilton, 1953.

Heffernan, Margaret. *Wilful Blindness: Why We Ignore the Obvious at Our Peril.* New York: Simon and Schuster, 2011.

Heng Swee Keat, "Working Towards Our Aspirations." In *Reflections of Our Singapore Conversation*, 4. 2013. Reach. Accessed 19 June 2017. https://www. reach.gov.sg/read/our-sg-conversation.

Hidalgo, César A., and Ricardo Hausmann. "The Building Blocks of Economic Complexity." *Proceedings of the National Academy of Sciences* 106, no. 26 (2009): 10570–75.

Huang, Natalia. "Singapore Should Have Wildlife Control Down to a Science." *The Straits Times*, 22 February 2015. Accessed 19 June 2017. http://www.straitstimes. com/opinion/singapore-should-have-wildlife-control-down-to-a-science.

Jacobs, Jane. *The Life and Death of Great American Cities*. New York: Random House, 1961.

Jagdish, Bharati. "Don't Blame the Govt; Take Ownership of Choices: Ground-Up Initiative's Tay Lai Hock." Channel NewsAsia, 9 July 2016. Accessed 14 June 2017. http://www.channelnewsasia.com/news/singapore/don-t-blame-the-govt-take-ownership-of-choices-ground-up-initiat-7903714.

Khanna, Parag. *Connectography: Mapping the Global Network Revolution*. London: Weidenfeld & Nicolson, 2016.

Lee, Hsien Loong. "National Day Rally 2016 Speech." Speech, ITE College Central, 21 August 2016. Prime Minister's Office. Accessed 13 June 2017. http://www. pmo.gov.sg/national-day-rally-2016-speech-english-part-2.

Lee, Hsien Loong. "Prime Minister Lee Hsien Loong's National Day Rally 2011 Speech (English)." Speech, National University of Singapore, 14 August 2011. Prime Minister's Office. Accessed 13 June 2017. http://www.pmo.gov.sg/newsroom/ prime-minister-lee-hsien-loongs-national-day-rally-2011-speech-english.

Lee, Hsien Loong. "PM Lee Hsien Loong at the Singapore Institute of Technology Dialogue with SITizens 2016." Speech, Singapore Institute of Technology, 24 October 2016. Prime Minister's Office. Accessed 16 June 2017. http://www. pmo.gov.sg/newsroom/pm-lee-hsien-loong-singapore-institute-technology-dialogue-sitizens-2016.

Lee, Hsien Loong. "Transcript of Prime Minister Lee Hsien Loong's Speech at the Official Opening of the Jurong Rock Caverns." Speech, Singapore, 2 September 2014. Prime Minister's Office. Accessed 8 June 2017. http://www.pmo.gov.sg/ newsroom/transcript-prime-minister-lee-hsien-loongs-speech-official-opening-jurong-rock-caverns.

Lee, Kuan Yew. "National Day Rally 1986 Speech." Speech, Kallang Theatre, Singapore, 17 August 1986. National Archives of Singapore. Accessed 13 June 2017. http://www.nas.gov.sg/archivesonline/audiovisual_records/record-details/ 48aabfb1-1164-11e3-83d5-0050568939ad.

Lee, Kuan Yew. "Speech by Prime Minister Lee Kuan Yew at his 60th Birthday." Speech, Mandarin Oriental Hotel, Singapore, 16 September 1983. National Archives of Singapore. Accessed 6 June 2017. http://www.nas.gov.sg/ archivesonline/data/pdfdoc/lky19830916.pdf.

Lee, Kuan Yew. "Summary of Speech by the Prime Minister at the 10th Anniversary Celebration of the Jalan Tenteram Community Centre." Speech, Jalan Tenteram Community Centre, Singapore, 27 June 1970. National Archives of Singapore. Accessed 14 June 2017. http://www.nas.gov.sg/archivesonline/ data/pdfdoc/lky19700627.pdf.

Lee, Kuan Yew. "Summary of the Case of the Singapore Government by the Prime Minister, Mr. Lee Kuan Yew, Disposing of Points Made by the Representatives of the 19 Singapore Assemblymen who Appeared Before the Committee Earlier in the Morning of the Same Day." Speech, Singapore, 13 August 1962. National Archives of Singapore. Accessed 13 June 2017. http://www.nas.gov. sg/archivesonline/data/pdfdoc/lky19620726c.pdf.

Long, Simon. "The Singapore Exception." *The Economist*, 18 July 2015. Accessed 13 June 2017. http://www.economist.com/news/special-report/21657606-continue-flourish-its-second-half-century-south-east-asias-miracle-city-state.

Lorenz, Edward. "Does the Flap of a Butterfly's Wings in Brazil Set Off a Tornado in Texas?" Paper presented at the Global Atmospheric Meeting 139th Meeting of the American Association for the Advancement of Science, Washington, DC, 29 December 1972.

Marx, Karl. *Grundrisse*. London: Penguin, 1973.

Meadows, Donella H., Dennis L. Meadows, Jørgen Randers, and William W. Behrens III. *The Limits to Growth*. New York: Universe Books, 1972.

Menon, Ravi. "Markets and Government: Striking a Balance in Singapore." Speech, Singapore Economic Policy Forum, Grand Hyatt, Singapore, 22 October 2010. Economic Society of Singapore. Accessed 13 June 2017. http://ess.org. sg/Events/Files/2010/R_Menon_speech.pdf.

Menon, Ravi. "Singapore's FinTech Journey — Where We Are, What Is Next." Speech, Singapore FinTech Festival — FinTech Conference, Singapore, 16 November 2016. Accessed 19 June 2017. http://www.mas.gov.sg/News-and-Publications/Speeches-and-Monetary-Policy-Statements/Speeches/2016/Singapore-FinTech-Journey.aspx.

Musk, Elon. "A Conversation with Elon Musk." Speech, World Government Summit 2017, Dubai, 13 February 2017.

Nathan, Sellapan Ramanathan, and Timothy Auger. *S R Nathan in Conversation.* Singapore: Editions Didier Millet, 2015.

Nielsen. "Total Audience Report: Q1 2016." Accessed 16 June 2017. http://www.nielsen.com/us/en/insights/reports/2016/the-total-audience-report-q1-2016.html.

Nisbett, Richard. *The Geography of Thought: How Asians and Westerners Think Differently... and Why.* New York: Simon and Schuster, 2010.

Osborne, David, and Ted Gaebler. *Reinventing Government: How the Entrepreneurial Spirit is Transforming the Public Sector.* Reading, Mass: Addison-Wesley, 1992.

Purba, Kornelius. "RI Asked to Continue Lead ASEAN Role." *The Jakarta Post*, 2 November 1998.

Rajaratnam, S. "Rajaratnam, S, 26 July 1982." Interview. National Archives of Singapore. Accessed 13 June 2017. http://www.nas.gov.sg/archivesonline/viewer?uuid=c8215047-1160-11e3-83d5-0050568939ad-OHC000149_015.

Rajaratnam, S. "Speech by Mr S Rajaratnam, Minister for Foreign Affairs." Speech, Science Centre, Singapore, 20 December 1979. National Archives of Singapore. Accessed 6 June 2017. http://www.nas.gov.sg/archivesonline/data/pdfdoc/SR19791220s.pdf.

Reynolds, Matthew. "'Land is so Yesterday': e-Residents and 'Digital Embassies' Could Replace Country Borders." *Wired*, 17 October 2016. Accessed 16 June 2017. http://www.wired.co.uk/article/taavi-kotka-estonian-government.

Rittel, Horst W. J., and Melvin M. Webber. "Dilemmas in a General Theory of Planning." *Policy Sciences* 4, no. 2 (1973): 155–169.

Rodin, Judith. *The Resilience Dividend: Managing Disruption, Avoiding Disaster, and Growing Stronger in an Unpredictable World.* London: Profile Books, 2014.

Romer, Paul. "Interview on Urbanisation, Charter Cities and Growth Theory." Interview transcript, interview with *iMoney Magazine*. 29 April 2015. Accessed 15 June 2017. https://paulromer.net/tag/charter-cities/.

Roosevelt, Franklin D. "Inaugural Address: Address by Franklin D. Roosevelt, 1933." Speech, Joint Congressional Committee on Inaugural Ceremonies, Washington, DC, United States, 4 March 1933. Accessed 8 June 2017. https://www.inaugural.senate.gov/about/past-inaugural-ceremonies/37th-inaugural-ceremonies/.

Rumsfeld, Donald H. "Department of Defense News Briefing." Transcript, 12 February 2002. Department of Defense. Accessed 6 June 2017. http://archive.defense.gov/Transcripts/Transcript.aspx?TranscriptID=2636.

Schelling, Thomas. "The Role of War Games and Exercises." In *Managing Nuclear Operations*, edited by Ashton Burton Carter, John D. Steinbruner, Charles A. Zraket, and Sherman Frankel, 426–444. Washington, DC: The Brookings Institution, 1987.

Schwab, Klaus. "The Fourth Industrial Revolution: What it Means, How to Respond." 14 January 2016. Accessed 8 June 2017. https://www.weforum.org/agenda/2016/01/the-fourth-industrial-revolution-what-it-means-and-how-to-respond/.

Schwartz, Peter. "Singapore: The Apple of Nations." *Ethos*: Issue 7, January 2010. Accessed 13 June 2017. https://www.cscollege.gov.sg/Knowledge/Ethos/Issue%207%20Jan%202010/Pages/Singapore-The-Apple-of-Nations.aspx.

Simon, Herbert A. *Models of Man; Social and Rational*. New York: John Wiley and Sons, 1957.

Singapore Legislative Assembly. *Debates III*. No. 20. 5 March 1957, col. 1,471.

Steffen, Will, Sanderson, Angelina, Tyson, Peter, Jäger, Jill, Matson, Pamela, Moore III, Berrien, Oldfield, Frank, Richardson, Katherine, Schellnhuber, H. John, Turner, B. L. II, and Robert J. Wasson. "Global Change and the Earth System: A Planet under Pressure." *Springer* (2003). Accessed 14 June 2017. http://www.igbp.net/download/18.56b5e28e137d8d8c09380001694/1376383141875/SpringerIGBPSynthesisSteffenetal2004_web.pdf.

Strouse, Jean. *Morgan: American Financier*. New York: Random House, 1999.

Taleb, Nassim Nicholas. *Antifragile: Things that Gain from Disorder. Incerto* series vol. 3. New York: Random House, 2012.

Taleb, Nassim Nicholas. *The Black Swan: The Impact of the Highly Improbable*. New York: Random House, 2007.

Tan, Gee Paw. *Singapore Chronicles: Water*. Singapore: Straits Times Press, 2016.

Tesla, Nikola. "When Woman is Boss." Interview by John B. Kennedy. *Colliers*. 30 January 1926. Accessed 19 June 2017. http://www.tfcbooks.com/tesla/1926-01-30.htm.

Tetlow, Gemma. "Treasury Made No Plans for Brexit, Says New Head Tom Scholar." *Financial Times, 7* July 2016. Accessed 12 June 2017. https://www.ft.com/content/f5797e2a-444d-11e6-b22f-79eb4891c97d?mhq5j=e3.

Tipping, Andrew, Andrew Schmal, and Frederick Duiven. "2015 Commercial Transportation Trends," *Pricewaterhouse Coopers*, 2015. http://www.strategyand.pwc.com/global/home/what-we-think/industry-perspectives/perspectives/2015-commercial-transportation-trends.

The Economist. "A Little Red Dot in a Sea of Green." Accessed 13 June 2017. http://
www.economist.com/news/special-report/21657610-sense-vulnerability-
has-made-singapore-what-it-today-can-it-now-relax-bit.

The Heritage Foundation. 2017 Index of Economic Freedom. (n.d.). Accessed 13
June 2017. http://www.heritage.org/index/country/singapore.

The Straits Times. "Some Who Thought Jurong was 'Goh's Folly,'" 22 May 1970.

Toffler, Alvin. *Future Shock.* Amereon: New York, 1970.

Turnbull, Constance Mary. *A History of Modern Singapore, 1819–2005.* NUS Press,
2009.

van der Heijden, Kees, Bradfield, Ron, Burt, George, Cairns, George, and Wright,
George. *The Sixth Sense: Accelerating Organizational Learning with Scenarios.*
West Sussex: John Wiley and Sons, 2002.

Willingham, Bill. *Super Team, Fables: Volume 16.* New York: Vertigo, 2011.

Yeo, George Yong-Boon, Asad Latif, and Huiling Li. *George Yeo on Bonsai, Banyan
and the Tao.* Singapore: World Scientific, 2015.

About the Cover Illustrator

Caleb Tan ("Bucketcaleb") is an illustrator from Singapore. He graduated from the School of Technology for the Arts, Republic Polytechnic in 2009. Caleb illustrated a Singapore children's book with Direct Life Foundation and AF Storytellers, which was launched in 2016. He works closely with the Organisation of Illustrators Council (Singapore).